OSPREY COMBAT AIRCRAFT • 8

P-61
BLACK WIDOW
UNITS OF WORLD WAR 2

SERIES EDITOR: TONY HOLMES

OSPREY COMBAT AIRCRAFT • 8

P-61
BLACK WIDOW
UNITS OF WORLD WAR 2

Warren Thompson

329

OSPREY
AVIATION

Front Cover
The Spook, a night stalking P-61 Black Widow assigned to the Iwo Jima-based 548th Night Fighter Squadron (NFS) and flown by Lt Melvin Bode and R/O Lt Avery J Miller, fires all of its guns at a 'Betty' bomber as it flees into the apparent safety of a cloud bank. The crews of Northrop's heavily armed nightfighter roamed the vast darkness above the Pacific Ocean waiting to acquire an unsuspecting Japanese bomber on radar as it attempted to penetrate the defences of forward allied air bases. The powerful all-black fighter possessed enough horsepower to readily overtake any contact it may encounter, and its armament of four .50 cal machine guns and four 20 mm cannon could swiftly depatch its target once 'locked on'. Indeed, most of the kills scored by the aircraft in the Pacific were achieved so quickly that enemy crews rarely knew what had hit them. 'Betty' bombers became a particular favourite of Black Widow units, as the aircraft would spectacularly explode when the P-61's 20 mm rounds impacted the Japanese aircraft's vulnerable fuel tanks
(*Cover artwork by Iain Wyllie*)

First published in Great Britain in 1998 by Osprey Publishing, Elms Court, Chapel Way, Botley, Oxford OX2 9LP, United Kingdom

ISBN 1 85532 725 2

Edited by Tony Holmes
Page design by Tony Truscott
Cover Artwork by Iain Wyllie
Aircraft Profiles and Nose Art by Mark Styling
Figure Artwork by Mike Chappell
Scale Drawings by Mark Styling

Printed in Hong Kong

EDITOR'S NOTE
To make this best-selling series as authoritative as possible, the editor would be extremely interested in hearing from any individual who may have relevant photographs, documentation or first-hand experiences relating to the elite pilots, and their aircraft, of the various theatres of war. Any material used will be fully credited to its original source. Please write to Tony Holmes at 10 Prospect Road, Sevenoaks, Kent TN13 3UA, United Kingom.

FOR A CATALOGUE OF ALL BOOKS PUBLISHED BY OSPREY PLEASE WRITE TO:
The Marketing Manager, Osprey Publishing Ltd.,
P.O. Box 140, Wellingborough, Northants NN8 4ZA, United Kingdom.

CONTENTS

PRELUDE TO COMBAT

Wars have been fought for thousands of years, and in most, if not all of these conflicts, combat has taken place almost exclusively during daylight hours. Night has always seemed to provide a time to rest and regroup. However, with the invention of the aeroplane, new battle tactics began to evolve, although it wasn't until the mid-1930s that the art of using aircraft to fight at night began to mature.

The Royal Air Force (RAF) and the Luftwaffe would have to claim the lion's share of the credit for perfecting this art during the final years of peace. As the advent of a second world war became more of a reality, the potential for delivering significant damage and destruction to an enemy at night increased greatly. This was a new facet to the art of waging war, and the United States was only an observer at the onset.

As early as 1940, Northrop took the lead in coming up with a design for an aircraft that could fight in this new nocturnal arena. The finished prod-

A YP-61 is seen undergoing various sundry tests over the mountains of northern California. There were 13 pre-production 'YPs' built, and they provided most of the critical data that would be incorporated into the P-61A. The first YP-61 flew on 6 August 1943 (*Nick Williams*).

Above and top
A visual clue as to just how much
firepower the Black Widow
possessed. Machine gun and cannon
fire was designed to converge
several hundred feet in front of the
fighter, resulting in the deadliest of
barrages. This test was carried out
at the Northrop factory
(*Roy Wolford*)

uct was not only one of the largest fighters built during World War 2, but it also proved to be the most devastating aircraft of its type to emerge from that era.

Northrop's new entry into the nightfighter business was an all-metal, twin boom, twin tail, monoplane. In terms of its sheer size, the aircraft boasted dimensions more suited to a medium bomber than a fighter – it was three times heavier than a P-51 and almost twice as heavy as the P-47. The P-61 was powered by two Pratt & Whitney R-2800 engines that developed over 2000 horsepower each, and with a comfortable combat range of over 1000 miles, it could cover a wide area and be available for instant high speed intercepts. Thanks to its 'long legs', the P-61 always worked alone.

During its initial production, the Black Widow was fitted with a top turret that housed four .50 cal machine guns and a dorsal fairing with four 20 mm cannon – the combination of this firepower and the aircraft's new radar put any enemy aircraft flying at night in harm's way!

This volume is about the P-61, and what it accomplished in a hostile environment. We have all read 'spell binding' accounts of daylight dogfights, and we can easily visualise just what the pilots' saw. It was always

An impressive line up of brand new P-61A-10s outside the Northrop assembly plant in Hawthorne, California. Exactly 100 A-10s were produced, and most saw combat. Note the camouflage netting in the right background (*Northrop*)

taken for granted that when you flew, the sky was bright and the visibility extended as far as one could see. Not so for the nightfighter.

It is hard to imagine what it must have been like to lock onto a target at 2500 ft in inky blackness, then move in close to attempt visual identification, only to have the enemy pilot start taking violent evasive action which resulted in an aggressive dogfight at all altitudes. Throughout the engagement, the only contact the pilot would have with his quarry was through the eyes of his radar operator, who would be verbally translating to him what he saw on his small radar screen.

A 20-minute pursuit may end up in a blinding fireball 800 ft in front of the pilot, leaving him with just three or four seconds to pull up to avoid being consumed by the resulting debris. Fighting within a black, invisible, void, the result of each intercept initially hinged on how good the ground control intercept (GCI) people were, and once the 'bogey' appeared on the P-61's airborne intercept scope, how well the pilot and radar operator communicated.

Each 'kill' was unique. The mission reports seemed repetitious and without excitement, but you can be assured that this image existed only on paper. They were all different, with the majority of them being a frustrating experience for the aircrews involved. If they had had the benefit of daylight, the end result would have been more impressive! According to records published in *The Development and Production of Fighter Aircraft* (TSEST-A7), the P-

'The Maestro'. John W Myers was Northrop's Chief Test Pilot for the P-61, and he took his knowledge and skills into the field to show young nightfighter pilots how to get the maximum performance out of the aircraft. His demonstrations are still vividly remembered to this day by those who experienced them (*John W Myers*)

61 was determined to be highly manoeuvrable – more so than any other USAAF fighter. It could have been a major 'player' as a day fighter too, but that was not role for which this highly-specialised aircraft had been developed. As a result, there were very few encounters between enemy fighters and the Black Widow during daylight hours, and of the few that took place, some are covered in detail in this text.

The resulting explosion of a 'bogey' at night is impressive, but the aircrews nevertheless still failed to see exactly what their 20 mm fire was doing to the target. Maj Carroll Smith (the USAAF's top nightfighter ace with seven kills) was one of the few P-61 pilots to claim a kill during daylight, and he describes in chapter four how his target (a Japanese 'Frank') disintegrated in front of his eyes following a burst of 20 mm fire.

Between December 1942 and August 1945, the United States Army Air Corps/Force trained a total of 35,000 day fighter pilots. By comparison, only 485 nightfighter crews were trained during the same period. With the former, most of the cycle was spent honing the pilot's individual proficiency and his ability to work in a group. It was just the opposite with the nightfighters, for each was expected to be proficient within his speciality, but the success of these nocturnal warriors depended on how well they worked as a team – as did their very existence.

When P-61As started reaching the forward areas, there was one glaring problem that initially cropped up which could not have

The four 20 mm cannon housed in the base of the crew nacelle are serviced prior to test firing. This photograph was taken at the Northrop factory in California soon after this particular P-61 had come off the final assembly line (*Northrop*)

Here, the turret dome has been removed in order to better show off the array of four .50 cal machine guns that have been installed in the XP-61. This view was taken during the early testing of the Black Widow (*Gerald Balzer*)

been anticipated beforehand. Young pilots were not sure of themselves in this new, heavy, fighter, and they expressed particular concern in respect to the P-61's single engine performance at low altitude or on take-off? The problem got so bad that it was having a detrimental effect on the performance of the crews in combat. There was a simple solution to this problem, however, and it took the form of Northrop's most experienced P-61 test pilot, John W Myers. A most gifted aviator, he could 'wring out' the Black Widow as if it were an agile 'hot-rod'. Here, he relates the measures taken to reassure the pilots in forward area;.

'We had to get out where the Black Widows were in a hostile environment. My own objective was to make this lethal weapon the easiest to fly and most "forgiving" aeroplane in history. It would prove to those kids who were going to fly it on a black night that they had every comfort and every aid we could give them. The programme dictated that I would get to an island base a few days after the two tech reps – Danny Collins and Scott Johnson – had supervised re-assembling the first aeroplane at that particular base. I would fly it, with a pilot sitting behind me in the gunner's station. Then we would trade places and I would ride with him. I would do this a few times with three or four of the squadron's pilots and then move on to another squadron.

'It was natural that those kids would think that a 35,000-lb aeroplane (a monster in those days) was not manoeuvrable. Also, there was great concern about the loss of control in the event of an engine failure, so I had a little "show-off" flight that I had practiced. It took about three minutes. Very short take-off roll, back across the deck at red-line 420 mph, loop down to the deck again in an Immelmann. Coming out of this manoeuvre, feather one engine on the way down to the deck, two slow rolls off the deck into the dead engine, approach and land short . . .'

From that demonstration on, the pilots viewed their aircraft as invincible, and they flew them with a confidence that they had never had before!

All instrumental in making the Black Widow the deadliest nightfighter of its generation, Northrop's elite group of four test pilots pose in front of an idling P-61A. They are, from left to right, John W Myers, Max Stanley, Harry Crosby and Alex Papana. Crosby was later killed in the first flight of the XP-79. Note the face peering though the open side canopy hatch (*Northrop*)

Myers had made a life-time impression on many of the pilots that had been fortunate enough to witness the demonstration. Capt Mark Martin, a 6th NFS pilot that flew *Midnight Belle*, commented in a letter he had written to John Myers many years after the war;

'. . . but most of all I want to repeat my thanks to you for the demonstration ride you gave me when our 6th squadron received our first P-61s at Kipapa Air Field on Oahu. I particularly recall when you spotted a flight of Navy fighters, dived to their level, feathered one engine, and passed the Grumman F4Fs while doing slow rolls!'

Lt Robert D Thum, a pilot who would fly the Northrop fighter off of Iwo Jima with the 549th NFS, recalls his first impressions while he was finishing up advanced training at a base in California;

'On the whole, we were very disappointed in the P-61. We had been led to believe that this "secret new nightfighter" would be about the hottest and fastest thing around . . . faster than the P-38 and more manoeuvrable than any single-engine fighter! When the first one arrived, it seemed to us to be slow and cumbersome, and certainly not the hot-shot black bullet that we had dreamed of! Evidently, the attitude of our guys caught someone's attention. One day, a P-61 landed at our base and a tall, lanky, civilian type climbed down the cockpit ladder. He was none other than Johnny Myers, Northrop's Chief Test pilot. We were very wary of anyone flying a military aircraft in civilian clothes. We met with him in the ready room. He told us he was there to show us how to get the most out of the P-61, and we would have to fly it like a fighter and not a bomber!'

By late 1944 Northrop had cranked up their production to significant levels. There are enough P-61Bs visible in this assembly line photo to equip a full nightfighter squadron (*Roy Wolford*)

A wide-angle view of the pilot's station in the XP-61. There would be numerous changes made in the cockpit before the aircraft reached production, including the provision of a windscreen (*Roy Wolford*)

The rear of the Black Widow's crew nacelle housed the radar observer's (R/O) compartment. This picture was taken in the spring of 1945 at Hammer Field, and shows the R/O's station in the P-61B (*Bob Hughes*)

'The first flight demo we witnessed proved to us that Myers was no ordinary pilot . . . he was superb! He had the aeroplane off the ground in an incredibly short roll, climbed abruptly, and as soon as the gear was tucked in he went into a steep climb. He was soon out of sight, but when next seen, he was on a steep approach with both props feathered! He landed in about 500 ft, rolled up to our astounded group and let off an ashen faced flight commander.

'When my turn came, he instructed me to be sure I was securely strapped in as we taxied out. Myers told me "You chaps must remember this is a fighter. You have the safest, most modern aeroplane built to date. You also have the best engines in the world, Pratt & Whitney R-2800s. Do not baby them! Use them to the utmost. They will not fail you. Keep full power on as long as you reasonably want to. It won't hurt the engines. Just fly the hell out of this aeroplane – it won't hurt you!"

'He then ran the engines up to full power, released the brakes, and when we hit 100 mph, he rotated and kept full power on, retracted the gear and pointed the nose straight up (it seemed). We performed a maximum rated climb at, as I remember, about 130 mph or so. Then he feathered the left engine in that maximum climb and did a full roll around that dead engine! He

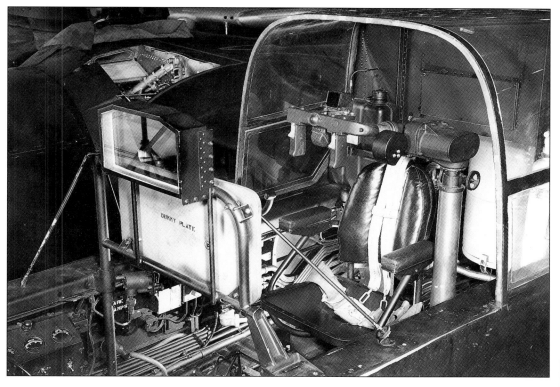

With the canopy removed, the gunner's station in the XP-61 is fully exposed. Note the sighting apparatus and the armour plating directly in front of him (*Northrop*)

levelled off, still with the left engine dead, and proceeded to make the tightest turns I have ever experienced into that dead engine. The P-61 bucked and stalled and dropped its nose . . . and still he pulled back on the yoke as hard as he could. All the aeroplane would do is complain and shudder and drop its nose automatically to pick up some more flying speed. Then he looped the aeroplane on one engine, shut down the right engine and in the quiet of that glider, he looped and rolled it. Lo and behold we were on the final, and he brought it in at 90 mph – both engines feathered – greased it on the runway and we were rolling off within 1000 ft! We were all believers!'

It took 15 P-61 airframes to develop, test and start production of the Black Widow. There were two XP-61s built, followed by thirteen YP-61s, and all of these aircraft were put through a very complicated test and evaluation regime. Nothing was left to chance by the test teams at Eglin Field. The need for the aircraft, and the optimism displayed by Northrop and the Air Corps, saw the Black Widow put into production *before* the final tests had been completed, resulting in several modifications being made to early production models on the assembly line.

Some 200 P-61As were manufactured, followed by 450 P-61Bs. The latter had most, if not all, of the 'bugs' worked out of the aircraft, and they would do an outstanding job until war's end. The C-model was in production when World War 2 ended, and none saw service outside of the USA. Northrop was well on its way to developing a long-range fighter escort for the B-29s bombing Japan when the surrender was announced, and work on the stillborn design, plus production of the P-61C, was immediately stopped in the wake of VJ-Day.

EUROPEAN THEATRE

As the Allied forces were gathering strength as part of the enormous build-up for D-Day, a new fighter began service with the Ninth Air Force. The result of almost three years of planning and testing, the aircraft performed its role far better than anything the enemy had, or would have, by war's end. It was the P-61 Black Widow.

The urgency of filling a void in the nightfighting arena had been felt by the RAF as far back as the bleak days of late 1940, when the Luftwaffe conducted a night *Blitz* on key British targets with near immunity. Northrop was alerted to developments in Europe, and they began working on the project immediately. At this time there were no indication that the United States would be drawn into the war, but the USAAC had nevertheless identified the need for such an aircraft, and that was all Northrop was waiting for.

Months before America was hit by the devastating attack on Pearl Harbor, high ranking RAF officers had visited the Northrop plant in California and relayed their combat experiences to the company designers, who duly took these comments into account when building the P-61.

In the year before the Black Widow became operational, the A-20 Havoc was converted into a 'stop gap' nightfighter. Although the bulk of its service, and effectiveness, was seen in the Pacific, a number were also used in Europe.

With the arrival of the first P-61As in the ETO, two nightfighter units were equipped with the Black Widow and placed under the control of the tactically-optimised Ninth Air Force. Both squadrons would muster up, receive their full complement of Black Widows and launch into combat from England. It was hoped that the units would be fully equipped and combat ready when D-Day rolled around, but this was not to be, for several minor delays slowed the P-61A's clearance for operations past 6 June 1944.

Nightfighter ace Lt Paul A Smith poses beside his *"Lady Gen"* (P-61A-5 42-5544) at the 422nd's base at Etain, in France, during the bitter winter of 1944/45. Aside from the six aircraft kill markings which adorn this veteran Black Widow, silhouettes denoting the destruction of five trains and a solitary V1 have also been painted beneath the cockpit (*Paul Smith*)

One of the more talented 'artists' within the 422nd NFS poses with his recently-completed masterpiece, *"Little Audrey"*. This nose art was applied to P-61B-15 42-39672, which was a rare attrition replacement aircraft that actually made it to a frontline unit. *"Little Audrey"* subsequently saw action with the 422nd squadron from bases in both France and Belgium (*Robert Danielson*)

The first P-61 squadron in the ETO was the 422nd NFS, and it formed in early March 1944 at Charmy Down, near Bath. The unit was well trained and ready to fight, but had no aircraft to fly! The 422nd initially shared its new home with fellow nightfighter squadron, the 423rd NFS, although the latter unit received a change of orders soon after arriving in the UK and re-equipped with the A-20J for night photographic work. This mission change came as a surprise at Charmy Down, and left the Ninth Air Force with just one unit ready to receive the P-61.

Orders were issued for the squadron to move en masse to Scorton, south of Newcastle, and this was duly carried out on 6 May. They would remain here until 25 July, with a detachment remaining on the south coast at Hurn aerodrome, near Bournemouth, until 11 July. All of this movement for a unit that had few aircraft was very frustrating! However, there was one uplifting note to all of this constant upheaval, for the detachment at Hurn got to work directly with No 125 'Newfoundland' Sqn, which was one of the best RAF nightfighter units in the business.

With the arrival of the 422nd's first P-61 on 23 May 1944 the unit's morale soared. Eight A-5s were delivered, and these were quickly brought up to operational status. It was originally stated that these aircraft would be ready for the squadron by 20 May, but a delay of three days seemed inconsequential after having been forced to 'kick their collective heels' since arriving in the UK almost three months before. All the 422nd NFS was interested in now was getting into combat.

None of the Black Widows issued to the 422nd had a top turret, for all of those built at the time were delivered to Boeing for fitment to the priority-listed B-29 Superfortress. The P-61's 'sting' was still lethal, however, thanks to its remaining quartet of 20 mm cannon. The downside to this situation was the transferring out of all the unit's redundant gunners.

The D-Day landings took place on 6 June 1944, and as the most monumental joint military effort in the history of warfare took place, an understrength 422nd NFS was forced to watch events unfolding from the sidelines. It was a difficult situation for these highly-trained crews to be caught up in, but there was nothing they could do . . . at least for the moment. Their chance would come in the weeks that followed, however.

Around the time of the invasion the squadron received enough aircraft to bring it up to an operational strength of 12, which allowed it start conducting its first training flights during the second week of June. However, the weather turned bad at the same time, with violent winds leading to pilots experiencing trim tab problems in flight – what a way to start a war! On 17 June the commanding officer of the squadron, Lt Col Orris B Johnson, received permission for the 422nd to start performing practice intercepts against RAF Halifax bomber crews that were also in the final stages of their training programme.

Just as things were at last progressing in the right direction, word reached the unit from Ninth Air Force high command that the P-61 would not be allowed to fly in combat as its performance was considered to be inferior to the RAF's Mosquito. The squadron went into a rage! Just

A close-up of Lt Paul Smith in the cockpit of his Black Widow. One the six swastikas stencilled onto this aircraft represented a probable kill, and it was eventually removed. Aside from being a noted locomotive 'killer', *"Lady GEN"* was also adorned with an impressive tally of lightning bolts, each of which denoted a completed mission (*Gerald Balzer*)

The 'heart and soul' of any nightfighter squadron was its groundcrews, who kept the Black Widows flying all night long on minimal stocks of spares. Three of the 'troops' from the 422nd take a break in order to show off their charge – P-61A *Midnight Menace*, which was operating from its temporary base in France at the time. Note the pierced steel planking (PSP) on which the big fighter is parked (*Bob Danielson*)

one life-line existed for the aircraft in the form of a fly-off between the P-61 and a Mosquito. The pilot chosen to uphold the Northrop fighter's honour, and thus preserve its place in history, was 1Lt Donald J Doyle. On 5 July both aircraft duly went through their 'demos', with their respective pilots adopting a 'balls to the wall' attitude. As every member of the 422nd had predicted, the P-61 excelled in every facet of the test – it was faster at 5000, 10,000 and 20,000 ft, out-turned the Mosquito at every altitude by a considerable margin and far surpassed it in rate of climb. All obstacles had finally been removed.

Eleven days later six P-61As departed Scorton for Ford airfield, on the Channel coast. The aircraft were going to do battle with the V1 'Buzz Bomb' – at last the new nightfighter was getting the opportunity to make its mark. These sorties against the unmanned bombs would be referred to as 'Anti-Diver' missions, the P-61s being drafted in response to the alarming increase in V1 attacks.

Future Black Widow ace 2Lt Herman E Ernst recalls his first and second missions, which were flown with his Radar Operator (R/O), Flt Off Edward H Kopsel;

'Over the English Channel on our first mission, we were cruising at 7500 ft when we spotted a "Diver" clipping along at 2000 ft. I dropped the nose of my '61 and pushed the throttle forward to close the gap as quickly as possible. The V1 was flying at 340 mph. All of a sudden there was a loud boom and a tremendous amount of noise in the cockpit. Kopsel was screaming into the intercom, but I could not understand a word. My first thought was that a German nightfighter had gotten in behind us and had shot us down . . . and on our very first mission!

Lt Col Oris B Johnson (the CO of the 422nd NFS) stands up in the cockpit of his distinctively-marked P-61 prior to flying a mission. On 24 October 1944 Johnson tangled with three Fw 190s at twilight during an evening sortie in this aircraft, shooting down one of the enemy fighters (*Fred Stegner*)

Lt Van A Neiswender runs up the engines of his P-61 at Etain in preparation for a mission later that night. *Daisy Mae* was assigned to this pilot throughout his tour (*Van Neiswender*)

'Seconds later I realised that the aircraft was still responding, although there was still a terrific amount of noise. I aborted the mission and flew back to Ford. After landing we discovered that the plexiglas tail cone had disintegrated due to the pressure. This problem was solved by fitting a flat piece of plexiglas over the opening.

'The next night we went up again, and it didn't take long to spot another "Diver". The scenario was similar to the previous night – dive down, line up behind and open fire. This time we closed the gap and fired several 20 mm rounds. They found their mark all over the propulsion unit and the bomb lost power, nosed over and went into the sea. This was to be the 422nd's first "kill" of the war!'

In the meantime, the second, and final, nightfighter squadron within the Ninth Air Force was also nearing operational readiness. The 425th NFS had arrived at Charmy Down on 26 May, and had followed the 422nd north to Scorton on 12 June, where it remained until 12 August. The unit had received its first P-61 on 15 June, but would take until the final days of July to receive enough aircraft to bring itself up to strength.

Like the 422nd, the 425th's aircraft were devoid of top turrets, which left an empty gunner's compartment – this was subsequently occupied by the R/Os after the unit had received permission to move them forward from the rear compartment to the gunner's station, which was immediately behind the pilot. This shift would work out well, for it brought the two crewmen into closer proximity with each other. Such an arrangement had been shown to increase crew effectiveness in the Mosquito.

Freshly painted invasion stripes stand out on a pair of then relatively new 422nd NFS Black Widows. This photograph was taken at a base in England soon after D-Day – and prior to the squadron receiving its full complement of aircraft. Framed under the booms of the aircraft in the foreground is Lt Herman Ernst's P-61A-5 42-5547 *"Borrowed Time"*. Both Ernst and his R/O, Edward Kopsel, went on to achieve ace status while flying this aircraft. Note the Mosquito being adorned with invasion stripes behind 42-5547, and the two Typhoons parked in the distance (*Herman Ernst*).

The 425th was commanded by Lt Col Leon G Lewis, who flew the much-photographed P-61A *WABASH CANNON-BALL IV*. As with the 422nd, the squadron's first foray into combat would be against the V1s, and they would shoot down their first on the night of 7 August. Lt Francis V Sartanowicz and his R/O, 2Lt Edward Van Sickel, were performing a routine patrol over the Channel when, at 0225, they saw the tell-tale plume of flame that denoted a V1 at an altitude of 3500 ft, heading for its target. It had already begun to lose height when visually acquired by the P-61 crew, and as Sartanowicz locked on behind it, the 'Buzz bomb's' speed was clocked at about 300 mph. Closing the gap posed no problem for the pilot, and the fighter's big R-2800 radials responded with a surge once the throttles had been opened up. The P-61 was also at a higher altitude, giving it a speed advantage as it dived on the V1.

When the gap had been closed to a very dangerous 600 ft, the pilot squeezed off a long burst of 20 mm cannon shell. They arced down and met perfectly with the 'Buzz Bomb's' propulsion unit, their impact separating the latter from the explosive warhead, which fell into the Channel and erupted in a giant fireball. It had been a lucky hit that could have easily resulted in the V1 exploding directly in front of the P-61, causing severe damage to the nightfighter.

Hunting at night was always dangerous, for the Germans were blessed with an abundance of skilled nightfighter crews and specialised aircraft types. However, if you had to select one target as being potentially the most dangerous to the P-61 from among several manned aircraft types and the unmanned V1, it had to be the latter, for an exploding V1, with its all-consuming fireball, could easily down a 'stalker'.

Indeed, there were several recorded incidents where the P-61 moved in too close and almost 'bought the farm'. One such episode involved 422nd pilot Capt Tadas J Spelis, and his R/O, Lt 'Lefty' Eleftherion. Fly-

High flying P-61As of the 422nd NFS form up over England in the wake of D-Day – the squadron failed to reach operational status in time to support the invasion of the continent. Leading the formation is shark-mouthed P-61A-5 42-5564 *Jukin' Judy* (USAF)

ing their regular aircraft (named *Katy THE KID*), the crew had been accompanied on this particular mission by the unit's intelligence officer, Lt Philip Guba, who occupied the empty gunner's seat. Their primary mission was to patrol a designated sector in the hope that they would come into contact with a German aircraft.

What they encountered instead was a V1, inbound to England at a slightly lower altitude. One of the crewmen stated that it looked 'like a full moon steaming along about three times faster than a freight train'. With an altitude advantage, Spelis turned the nose of his Black Widow straight at the V1, achieving an incredible closure speed. At 1500 ft Eleftherion called for Spelis to shoot, although the latter ignored his prompting, replying that he was going to make sure that the target didn't get through. As he remained transfixed with the gunsight, his closure continued. This was all happening in a matter of seconds . . . 1000 ft . . . 700 ft. Finally, at 400 ft Spelis triggered a burst from his cannons and all hell broke loose.

Instantly, there was a tremendous orange flash and the bomb went up like a gasoline storage dump. Guba later stated;

'It blew into a million pieces. Just before we fired, it looked like a massive neon watermelon, hurtling at us as if it were on invisible rails! Spelis was blinded by the light and we immediately started into a steep dive. It was a miracle that he was able to level us off before we hit the ground. The left rudder was burned off, as was the left aileron and half the left elevator. There was burned fabric dangling from everything when we landed.'

With a primary role of protecting frontline forces and high value assets behind friendly lines from marauding German aircraft, it was only a matter of time before the P-61 units were posted to France. The 422nd was the first to move from English soil when they made a brief flight across the Channel to the French airfield at Maupertus (A15) on 25 July – their sister squadron was posted further east to Vanne on 18 August. Neither outfit managed to properly settle in and get comfortable at their new sites because of the fluidity of the frontline, the 422nd soon moving firstly to Chateaudun and then Florennes, in Belgium, on 16 September. Likewise, the 425th had shifted to Le Moustier and then on to Coulommiers by 13 October.

Leading by example throughout this period of massive upheaval, 422nd NFS CO, Lt Col Johnson, was always in the thick of the action in his colourful P-61A, *No Love! NO NOTHING!* For example, late in the afternoon of 24 October, he and his R/O, Capt James Montgomery, took off from their base in Belgium, for a twilight patrol over enemy lines near Aachen. At precisely 1805 hours, GCI checked in and informed them of several enemy aircraft approaching from the east at 4000 ft. Descending from his patrol height of 10,000 ft, Johnson investigated the contact and, upon seeing no aircraft, immediately returned to his original 'perch'.

Minutes later, GCI notified them once again that they were picking up multiple 'bogies', this time at 5000 ft. Johnson dropped down a second time and soon spotted the elusive contacts – three Fw 190s loaded with bombs. Flying a straight and level course at about 250 mph, the German aircraft were soon engaged by Johnson, who flew right into their formation. Two of the fighter-bombers broke off and scattered, leaving the Black Widow pilot to focus on the lead Fw 190. Closing to 1000 ft, dead astern of the German aircraft, Johnson opened fire with two short bursts. Strikes were observed on the Fw 190's right wing as it drifted into a slow turn to the left. By this time the range had closed through 500 ft, and Johnson's thumb increased pressure on the firing button, letting fly a long five-second burst at literally point-blank range.

Fatal hits were observed all over the fuselage and engine, black smoke billowing out from the engine as the aircraft fell off into a vertical dive. At 2000 ft the pilot made a doomed effort to pull out but the Fw 190 hit the ground and exploded. By this time Johnson was so low that he had noticed light 'friendly' ground fire detonating around him. Swiftly climbing out of the flak band, he continued his patrol for a further 15 minutes before returning to base – where it was discovered that his aircraft had sus-

Pilot 1Lt John W Anderson (left) poses in front of his P-61A-5, 42-5543 *Tennessee "Ridge Runner"*, with one of the 422nd's senior enlisted men. The team of Anderson and Mogan shot down two German aircraft and a V1 during their combat tour (*John Anderson*)

Tennessee "Ridge Runner" was one of the many 422nd NFS Black Widows that scored kills during its long spell in the frontline. The weathered condition of the aircraft's invasion stripes suggest that it was probably also one of the first P-61s delivered to the squadron just prior to it being declared operational soon after D-Day (*John Anderson*)

The canteen truck, and its Red Cross 'girls', was always a welcome sight for the airmen that were isolated at bases in the country. RAF types and members of the 422nd NFS pose together with the girls for a photograph. To the left of the two ladies is future ace Lt Herman Ernst (*Fred Stegner*)

tained minor damage from the small arms fire. This engagement was one of only a handful fought between Black Widows and enemy fighters during daylight hours, the 422nd's official records showing that they achieved three confirmed kills over Fw 190s (all between 21 October and 17 December 1944).

The move into Belgium provided the 422nd with their biggest break, for they found themselves in a veritable 'feeding frenzy' due to the heavy nocturnal activity conducted by Luftwaffe bombers (principally Ju 87s, Ju 88s and Ju 188s) as they attempted to stem the advance of the Allied armies. 422nd pilot Capt Robert Elmore and his R/O, 2Lt Leonard Mapes, emerged as one of the most effective crews of this period, flying P-61A 42-5534 *'SHOO-SHOO-BABY'*.

At 0313 hours on 17 December 1944, Elmore and his R/O were assigned to patrol a sector that buffered the area between VII Corps' positions and the Rhine – the ground fighting had finally reached German soil. As expected, the weather was both cold and clear, and GCI was particularly busy because of the heavy enemy activity in the area. Capt Elmore recalls;

'We were vectored toward several "bogies", but we were unable to get close enough to obtain a positive visual and shoot at them. Then "Marmite" (GCI's call sign) vectored us towards an intruder just four miles away and below us. After letting down in a wide orbit to avoid overshooting, we "locked-on" with our airborne radar. The target was four-and-a-half miles ahead of us. I gave the 'Widow more throttle and rapidly closed

the distance down to about 1000 ft. At this distance we got a visual, but not a positive one, so we rolled on in to 500 ft. At this point we had him identified as a Ju 88.

'It was on a heading of 270°, flying at 4000 ft. His speed was constant at about 200 mph. Knowing full well what our 20 mm cannon could do, I eased to within 100 ft dead astern and pressed the firing button. After a quick burst, there was a bright white explosion from within the aircraft's fuselage. Maintaining my position, I fired a much longer burst of 20 mm that walked across his engines – fire immediately erupted from both. For some reason or another, the Ju 88 went into a slight nose up attitude. Then it fell away to its left side and nosed straight down. By now it was consumed in a fireball, finally exploding as it hit the ground. No parachutes were sighted. Checking my watch, it had been exactly 17 minutes since GCI had given us the contact.'

Elmore and Mapes were one of the top-scoring teams within the ranks of the 422nd, finishing the war with four confirmed kills (a Ju 88, Bf 110 and two Ju 52s) and one V1 to their credit. They came close to, and perhaps should have achieved, 'acedom' on 16 December, when they were directed in behind what they identified as a Ju 88. At the extreme limits of their range, and low on fuel, the crew pulled in behind the target, poured a stream of 20 mm into it and seconds later saw two parachutes. With time running out, Elmore had to turn back to base, so there was no confirmation of the aircraft hitting the ground or actually going down. It is almost certain that they should have been listed as the 422nd's fourth ace team.

The Ju 88 was considered by many to be the Luftwaffe's most versatile wartime aircraft. Its capabilities were numerous, and included the role of nightfighter.

It is the late autumn of 1944, and the 425th NFS has set up their operating base at Coulommiers (A58), in France. The groundcrew has stopped working on the hydraulic system for the P-61's right main gear in order to pose for the camera (*Van Neiswender*)

This photo serves as stark testimony to what could happen to a P-61 when it got too close to a German V1 before firing. During the attack 20 mm cannon rounds missed the propulsion unit and hit the warhead. With no time to evade, the pilot of the Black Widow had to fly right through the fireball, which almost brought him down. The charred fighter belonged to the 422nd NFS (*Fred Stegner*)

The Ju 88 also went through a complete redesign midway through the war, resulting in the larger Ju 188. The latter could easily operate at ceilings above 27,000 ft at speeds in excess of 270 mph, and being one of the most prominent weapons in the Luftwaffe's arsenal in the final year of the war, a substantial number of them fell victim to the P-61's guns. Forced to fly at much lower altitudes and slower speeds than they were originally designed for in an attempt to provide aerial support for the beleaguered ground troops, the Ju 188 proved to be easy prey for the Black Widow.

The Germans unleashed their final major attack in the west through the Ardennes forest in mid-December 1944, this large-scale assault becoming known as the 'Battle of the Bulge'. In the air, the Luftwaffe did its best to support the counter-attack by striking at Allied troop emplacements at night, and it was whilst responding to these missions that the 422nd NFS became the top-scoring nightfighter squadron of the USAAF. The battle commenced on the night of 16 December, the Germans' timing proving to be spot on when it came to factoring in the effectiveness of the two American nightfighter squadrons.

The bad weather in the area had persisted for 29 days leading up to the attack on the 16th, allowing the Germans to effectively mass their forces without hindrance from the air. Allied reconnaissance aircraft had struggled to complete crucial sorties during this period, with visibility being so bad that detecting German tank and troop movements had been an all but impossible task. Further adding to the poor Allied intelligence picture, all enemy movements had been made under the cover of darkness.

The weather was not the only factor in the Germans' favour, for both the 422nd and 425th NFSs were severely handicapped by a lack of sufficient aircraft. This had been caused by a major spares shortage, resulting in both units having just ten serviceable aircraft apiece available – this

Christened *Battle Ax* (the name was worn on the right side of the forward fuselage), this 422nd P-61 carried the scoreboard of 1Lt Eugene D Axtell below its cockpit. As the five swastikas reveal, he was one of three aces produced by this high-scoring squadron (*John Anderson*)

Flt Off Chet Hawley (left) and his pilot, 2Lt James Postlewaite, pose by their P-61, *Little Linda*, at the 422nd's new French base at Maupertus (A15) in late July 1944 – note the variation in their clothing. The squadron's war on the V1 was now all but over, and shortly after this photograph was taken, the 422nd scored its first kill against a manned German aircraft (*John Anderson*)

The crew of *"Double Trouble"* (P-61A-10 42-5565) are suited up ready for a mission out of their base in France. On the left is 1Lt Robert G Bolinder and on the right his R/O, 2Lt Robert F Graham, and they are standing next to John Anderson's P-61A-5 42-5543 *Tennessee "Ridge Runner"* (*John W Anderson*)

number could not effectively police such a vast area.

Official Air Corps records state that what few Black Widow crews the 422nd could get airborne during the first week of December all reported an unusually large number of 'hooded' head lights on the roads. By the night of 6/7 December, these lights were no longer shielded, and some followed the road patterns while others were at random. The latter probably represented tanks and tracked vehicles that were not restricted to the roads. The sightings, combined with accelerated train activity, had further increased by the 12th/13th.

Right after the all-out attack had commenced, the 422nd sent all available P-61s out to hit the marshalling yards at Rheinbach, Gemund and Schleiden – no significant results were recorded. Parallel to the 422nd's operating area, the 425th had been attempting to perform a similar mission. They too had reported similar increased movements, the most alarming of which were the large motor convoys sighted around Traben Trarbach, Homburg, Neunkirchen and Kaiserslautern.

On one of these night, 425th NFS pilot Lt Alvin 'Bud' Anderson (flying P-61 *Dangerous Dan*) put his cannon to good use against locomotives;

Again wearing a wide variety of clothing and flying gear, these four individuals, seen in the early autumn of 1944, comprise two complete nightfighter crews within the 422nd, namely (from left to right) Lt John W Anderson and Lt James W Mogan (*Tennessee "Ridge Runner"*), and Capt Robert Elmore and his R/O, Leonard Mapes (*'Shoo-Shoo-Baby*)
(*Robert Elmore*)

'We took to train busting rather quickly, although it was dangerous. This was because the engine could blow up right in your face, severely damaging your aircraft, or worse. On one cold night, my R/O, Lt John Smith, and I were on a routine patrol in our designated sector. Flying at 15,000 ft with nothing on the scope, we were watching for any sign of movement on the ground.

'Suddenly, we spotted what appeared to be a large convoy about 15 miles east of us. I immediately "split-S'd" straight down to about 500 ft. We were deep inside German territory, so there was absolutely no hesitation on my part. I went across the line of moving objects with all four 20 mm cannon blasting. Completing the first pass, we both realised we had stumbled upon a major marshalling yard. I pulled up abruptly, wheeled around and lined up for another pass. There were four locomotives spouting steam and, in his haste to abandon his engine, one of the engineers had failed to cut his headlights. Con-

422nd NFS pilots Lt Eugene Lee (the pilot of the aircraft in the photo, *Jukin' Judy*) and Lt Don J Doyle (*John W Anderson*)

centrating on this bright light, I fired another long burst.

'Focusing on the light had mesmerised me. I was brought back to reality by the screaming in my headset. It was my R/O. I snapped out of it and pulled up in time. At that moment, the locomotive exploded. The violent force sent us several thousand feet straight up! I fought with the controls until I could get everything squared away. The next thing on the agenda was to call GCI and tell them about this target, so the bombers could hit it during the day.'

When the reconnaissance aircraft returned with their film the next

morning, it revealed that Anderson had destroyed five locomotives. It also showed that he had stumbled onto the massive rail complex at Kaiserslautern.

By the time the 'Battle of the Bulge' commenced, the night patrol sectors for the P-61s were deep inside Germany, leaving very little airspace that was completely safe for the enemy to move at night.

Over Belgium, the weather had been so bad in December that the numbers of sorties flown by all aircraft had decreased by about 50 per cent. This figure was much greater for both of the nightfighter units, although for them spares, rather than weather, had been the problem. Serviceability rates got no better in the New Year either, the 422nd completing just 35 sorties for the entire month!

One of the more fortunate aircrews to get in some serious flying time during December was Lt John W Anderson and his R/O, 2Lt James W Mogan, who were assigned P-61A 42-5543 *TENNESSEE "RIDGE RUNNER"*. On the night of 25 December they were patrolling an assigned area over V Corps between the bomb line and the Rhine when GCI radioed that they had a 'bogey' at 20 miles heading west. Within minutes, Anderson had closed to airborne intercept (AI) range, and at three miles the R/O took over the chase. At 2500 ft they positively identified the target as a Ju 188, its fuselage silhouette and pointed wingtips giving it away.

Pulling up to the 12 o'clock position dead astern, Anderson opened up with his 20 mm cannon at a separation distance of 600 ft. The burst scored multiple strikes on the right wing root, causing the Ju 188 to gently bank to the left. A second burst detonated the right engine, smearing

Two talented craftsmen from the 422nd follow an assembly line technique in the production of hand-painted leather squadron emblems. These would be sewn onto the leather A2 flight jackets of the aircrews (*Fred Stegner*)

With the addition of bomb shackles and rockets beneath the wings of the P-61, the 425th NFS added the night intruder role to its mission brief. This photo was taken at Etain, in France (A82), in early 1945 (*USAF*)

The bitter winter of 1944/45 had very little effect on P-61 operations, crews simply donning extra layers of clothing to stave off the cold. Displaying appropriate dress sense, pilot, Capt Tadas Spelis (left), and his R/O, Lt Elutherios Eleftherion, pose in front of their aircraft, *Katy The Kid*, prior to climbing aboard for a night sortie (*John W Anderson*)

oil all over the canopy of the pursuing Black Widow. The enemy aircraft began to rapidly lose altitude, and seconds later it hit the ground and exploded – no parachutes were seen. Prior to this kill, Anderson had been observing the flashes on the ground caused by Allied artillery, duelling with its German counterpart. It wouldn't have been a good place to force-land!

Squadron records show that after five months of operational flying, the 422nd NFS had received only one replacement aircraft. Further entries reveal that as a result of this paucity of replacement P-61s, the unit had just four airworthy aircraft available at a time when German ground activity was at its peak, and each of these Black Widows was logging three to four missions a night. Other 'down' P-61s were being cannibalised for parts in order to keep the remaining few airborne, and every aircraft in the 422nd's inventory had in excess of 300 combat hours on its airframe.

The most critical component of the Black Widow's effectiveness was its radar, and the lack of parts, and resulting reduced efficiency of each set, had jeopardised the potency of those few aircraft that remained airworthy. The 425th was experiencing identical problems, for in the overall scheme of things pertaining to the final push for victory, the availability of spares for nightfighters just did not rate a very high priority. There were thousands of Allied aircraft being used on a daily basis over the entire European theatre, and two squadrons of P-61s that had less than a dozen workable aircraft between then were not in line for any major attention.

The impact of the Allies lacking a viable nightfighter force during the 'Battle of the Bulge' was validated at the end of the war by Germans that had been captured in the early spring of 1945. They stated that the freedom of movement they enjoyed at night during the battle had been a significant factor in the offensive's prolonged success. If the P-61s had been able to maintain a 90 per cent in-service rate during these critical months, the enemy would have paid a high price in manpower and equipment, plus lost the element of surprise for their counter-attack.

Despite crippling spares shortages, the 422nd somehow managed to achieve an improved sortie rate for a short period over Christmas, during which time its crews scored 11 confirmed kills over a four-day

period (24th to the 27th). One very unusual mission was recorded by ace Lt Herman Ernst and his R/O, Lt Edward Kopsel. They were flying their assigned Black Widow, 42-5547 *"BORROWED TIME"*, with squadron intelligence officer Lt Phillip Guba once again 'along for the ride' in the empty gunner's seat;

'We were flying at 8000 ft in a westerly direction toward our base. Lt Guba noticed an aircraft below us at 2000 ft with its red and yellow navigation lights on. New to me, it was dropping flares! I peeled off and quickly reached the unidentified "bogie", approaching from the rear. I pulled in behind him to a distance of about 1500 ft. With the help of the night glasses, Lt Guba was able to positively identify the aircraft as a Ju 88. By this time, the enemy aircraft had altered course to true north and was flying straight and level at 2000 ft at 250 mph.

'At that moment we were spotted, and the German pilot initiated violent evasive action. I still had him in my sights and the gap was steadily closing. From 500 ft directly behind, I gave him a burst. I observed many hits over the target's fuselage. The '88's dorsal turret opened up on us as I moved over to the right side to avoid overshooting. I dropped slightly low and lining him up again, squeezed off three short bursts. The hits caused both of the Ju 88's engines to explode and the aircraft fell away to the left and down. It impacted with the ground in a huge ball of fire. A second before it hit, I vividly remember seeing it fire off another red flare!'

By this stage the 425th was well entrenched at Etain, in France. They had moved in on 9 November, and would remain here until 12 April 1945. The location of this base provided them with access to virtually all of Germany, and most of their kills would be scored from here. As the number of sorties increased, so too did the Luftwaffe's aggressive night flying techniques, as 425th pilot Lt Van Neiswender witnessed at firsthand. He engaged a Me 410 on a night mission which he believes was flown by one of the most skilled adversaries he ever encountered. Neiswender, and his R/O, 2Lt David Parsons, were flying P-61A *Daisy Mae* above Bastogne at the time of the interception;

'I remember a full moon and excellent visibility that night. The first two hours of our mission were uneventful, then we received a message from GCI telling us of a "bogey" in the area. We were vectored in close enough to get an airborne intercept (AI) lock, but as soon as we had him on our scope, he did a near half-roll and dived for the dark woods below. I pushed the throttles wide open and the chase was on. This guy was absolutely fearless!'

'We stayed close, but not close enough to fire our guns, unfortunately.

Right up until war's end, P-61 groundcrews had to endure poor working conditions at austere airfields that, for the most part, lacked intact hangers – most sites in France and Germany had been heavily bombed by Allied aircraft prior to occupation. This 425th NFS Black Widow is undergoing field maintenance at a base in France in the late autumn of 1944 (*Van Neiswender*)

Pilot Lt Robert Yule (left) and R/O Lt Al Innerarity (middle) stand by *TABITHA*, alias P-61A-10 42-5569 of the 425th NFS, on the evening of 27 September 1944. This machine was not their regular aircraft. In November this crew was shot down while flying another P-61, Innerarity being killed in the subsequent crash (*Stan Woolley*)

We positively identified the enemy aircraft as an Me 410. I glanced down at my indicated airspeed and figured the '410 was exceeding 400 mph, because he was pulling away from us quickly. Although I had my fighter wide open, it was as if we were standing still. At that time, we lost all radar contact with the aircraft. We had also lost the tail cone at the rear of the R/O compartment as it caved in from the immense pressure created by the diving airspeed. Parsons was sitting behind me in the gunner's station, so there was no problem with his safety.'

The mission had lasted for a long three hours and ten minutes, and had resulted in nothing but frustration.

An interesting fact that is recorded in the 422nd history pertains to a report that summed up all nightfighter activity within Ninth Air Force confines for the month of December 1944. It stated that RAF nightfighter squadrons achieved 20 confirmed kills for the month, and that the 422nd had scored 18 victories during the same period. The latter figure is quite outstanding when you consider the small number of aircraft that the NFSs had to work with. If both units had had their full complement of P-61s serviceable it might have been a 'turkey shoot'.

As 1945 rolled around, war's end appeared nearer with each passing day. The only factor that was slowing the pace of the Allies was the weather. For the 422nd, January belonged to future squadron ace 1Lt Eugene D Axtell and his R/O, Lt John U Morris, for they scored every kill credited to the unit during this month, including the first aerial victory recorded by the USAAF in 1945 – they were directed in behind a Ju 88, which Axtell promptly filled full of holes, causing it to crash in a ball of flame. One of the quickest kills made by a Black Widow aircrew, the shoot down was recorded at 0300 on the morning of 1 January 1945.

By this late stage in the war, Allied aircraft had begun to encounter the Luftwaffe's most potent nocturnal weapon, the Me 262 jet nightfighter. Back in July 1944 the first jet day fighters had been engaged, and from time to time, these aircraft appeared in plain view and 'mixed it' with both the fighter escorts and the 'heavies'. Operating alongside the Me 262 in far smaller numbers was the rocket-powered Me 163 Komet, which Allied Intelligence believed had a top speed of around of 600 mph. It was much faster than any defending USAAF or RAF fighter, but possessed a woefully inadequate range. Usually seen around the Leipzig area, the Komet posed a definite threat to daylight fighters and bombers in 1945.

On the night of 15 November 1944 the team of Elmore and Mapes again recorded a first – a nighttime visual confirmation on a night flying Me 163. Lt Mapes remembers it well;

'We were flying what was known as a "free-lance" intruder mission around Bonn, Germany. It was around 2300 hours before we hit our area. The overcast was at 4000 ft, with a beautiful moonlit clear sky above.

Suddenly, I picked up a "bogey" on my radar that was high above us and travelling at a terrific speed. Just as it was about to pass over us, Elmore put us into a hard 180° turn. I could not find it on the radar and looked out above us. The sight was unbelievable! It appeared to be shaped like a wedge of pie with a long plume of flame coming from its rear end.

'I kept watching him and calling out where he was over the intercom. He appeared to be in a tight circle directly above us. About the time that Elmore got a visual, the flame died down to a glow and it started to spiral down on us. I could see intermittent bursts of fire from the nose, and knew it was cannon or machine gun fire. I relayed this on and we began taking violent evasive action. Suddenly, this strange aircraft broke off and went into a vertical climb, with a long plume of flame shooting out the rear end. After several manoeuvres like this, we both agreed that it was the new German Me 163 rocket plane. We never could get in a position to fire on it because of its tight spiralling and rapid climbs. Finally, it left the area and we never saw it again. Although we never fired a shot at it, it was a very memorable mission!'

This had been the first nocturnal sighting of the Komet by an American nightfighter squadron.

During the final months of war the Luftwaffe desperately tried new tactics and weaponry, with mixed results. One of the more successful programmes saw the Ju 88 fitted with unguided rockets in an effort to attack the bomber formations with a well placed barrage – the combination duly became the deadliest weapon yet devised to counter the bombers.

Of the 43 kills recorded by the 422nd NFS, nine were Ju 88s – the 425th was also able to achieve a rare victory over a Ju 88 nightfighter. Another night intruder that was up in significant numbers at this time was the Ju 188, the 422nd downing six during the 'Battle of the Bulge'.

One of these fell to 1Lt Paul Smith and his R/O, 1Lt Robert Tierney, on the night of 26 December 1944 during a routine patrol between Meuse and St Vith-Monschau. Due to the levels of activity that had been recorded over the previous nights, the crew knew that scoring opportuni-

With the cold weather approaching, groundcrews work out in the open at the 425th's base at Coulommiers on 10 October 1944. The large tent next to the parking area belonged to the armament section (*John Birmingham*)

Diminutive Hollywood legend Mickey Rooney dons flight gear before participating in a photo session with several members of the 422nd NFS. He was touring with an entertainment group that was visiting numerous military bases at the time (*John W Anderson*)

ties would likely arise during their sortie in regular mount P-61A-5 42-5544 *"Lady GEN"*, operating from strip A78 at Florennes, in Belgium.

Forty minutes into the patrol, GCI picked up an intruder at 7000 ft. They closed rapidly and overshot, identifying the 'bogey' as a Ju 188 as the raced passed it, losing the element of surprise in the process. The enemy pilot swiftly took violent evasive action by changing the direction of his flight every few second, diving, weaving and constantly altering his altitude. However, Smith was able to stay close to his quarry, and it was just a matter of time before the Ju 188 was destroyed.

Slowly reducing the gap down to about 500 ft, Smith took his chance with a 60° deflection shot when the target made a hard turn to port. His aim was good, and cannon shells ripped through the canopy glazing and destroyed the bomber's cockpit. The aircraft shuddered and then straightened out. Smith hit it again, this time with a 30° deflection shot, which impacted all over the starboard wing root and started a fire. The Ju 188 went into a gentle climb for a few seconds, then fell off on the damaged wing. The altitude of the fight had rapidly deteriorated as it had progressed, and the bomber soon hit the ground and exploded – the victorious crew later noted in their mission report that the Ju 188 was fitted with bomb racks, which were empty.

Having tasted success, the crew of *"Lady GEN"* went in search of further targets. About an hour after downing the Ju 188, GCI sent the P-61 up to 17,000 ft to check out an unidentified aircraft. Closing in from behind and underneath, the visual proved it to be a B-17, so they broke off and resumed their patrol once again. Shortly afterwards they were vectored on to another unidentified contact flying at 9000 ft – an altitude more associated with enemy raiders. Coming in too fast, they once again overshot the contact, which proved to be yet another Ju 188. Quickly turning back into the target, the P-61 closed up astern of the bomber to a separation distance of just 500 ft. Smith opened fire with a slight deflection shot that went wide, and the German pilot immediately peeled off to starboard, before completing a 'split-S' to port.

Over the next few minutes the dogfight 'bounced' up and down between 9000 ft and 500 ft, with visual contact being gained and lost three times. Smith finally found himself in a slight dive, allowing him to get off a short burst which found its mark. The first rounds peppered the fuselage, setting the bomber alight, whilst a second longer burst fired from just 300 ft dead astern caused the Ju 188's right engine to explode, blowing the right wing off outboard of the powerplant. Now in an uncontrollable spiral, the enemy aircraft hit the ground and exploded – it was also noted that this aircraft was fitted with bomb racks. Two kills in a matter of two hours proved not only to be Smith and Tierney's best ever return, but it also gave them their fourth and fifth kills – and coveted 'ace status'.

The 425th NFS ended the war with ten confirmed kills over manned aircraft, plus four V1s destroyed over the English Channel. The top 'Buzz Bomb' killer was Lt Garth Peterson with two, followed by Lt Francis Sartanowicz and Lt James Thompson with one apiece. The 422nd enjoyed success against the V1s too, 'bagging' five split between five crews.

The 422nd NFS was also the top-scoring American nightfighter outfit, period, downing 43 manned aircraft – no other P-61 squadron would come close to matching this tally. The totals for both ETO squadrons would have been significantly better had there been plenty of spare parts available, for the targets were certainly out there to be had. Of course the same 'ifs' applied to those day fighter squadrons grounded by the bad winter weather in late 1944 and early 1945.

The 425th deactivated on 25 August 1945, although it was later redesignated as the 317th All Weather Squadron. The 422nd was permanently deactivated on 30 September 1945.

During the 'Battle of the Bulge', the heavy snowfall created major problems for both the Allies and the Germans. This line-up shows 422nd and 414th NFS Black Widows after they had been dug out of the snow at Florennes (A78), in Belgium, during the winter of 1944/45 (*Paul Smith*)

NOSE ART

This three-page nose art section has been specially created by profile artist Mark Styling in order to better illustrate some of the more colourful art-works applied to the P-61s by their crews. Fully detailed commentaries for these pages can be found in the appendices.

26

33

27

34

30

35

28

Capt. C.D. Bourque

36

31

29

37

32

36

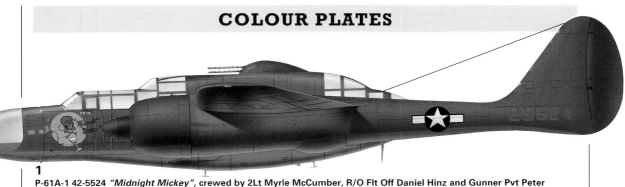

1
P-61A-1 42-5524 *"Midnight Mickey"*, crewed by 2Lt Myrle McCumber, R/O Flt Off Daniel Hinz and Gunner Pvt Peter
Dutkanicz, 6th NFS, Saipan, mid-1944

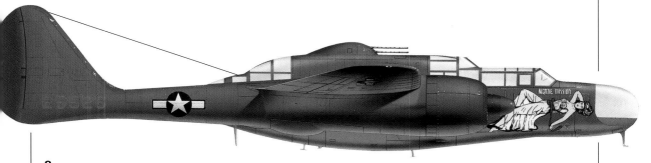

2
P-61A-1 44-5526 *NIGHTIE MISSION*, 6th NFS, Saipan, mid-1944

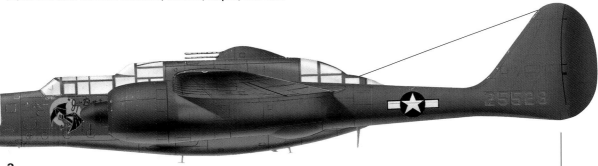

3
P-61A-1 44-5528 *"Jap Batty"*, crewed by 1Lt Francis Eaton, R/O 2Lt James Ketchum and Gunner S/Sgt William Anderson,
6th NFS, Saipan, November 1944

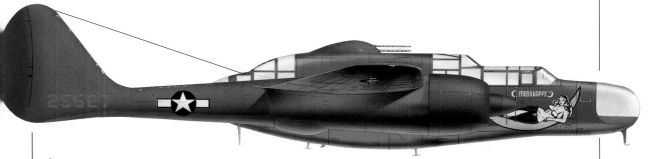

4
P-61A-1 44-5527 *MOONHAPPY*, crewed by 2Lt Dale 'Hap' Haberman, R/O Lt Raymond Mooney and Gunner Pvt Pat
Farelly, 6th NFS, Saipan, late 1944

5
P-61A-5 42-5554 *THE VIRGIN WIDOW*, crewed by 2Lt Robert Ferguson, R/O 2Lt Charles Ward and Gunner Sgt Leroy Miozzi, 6th NFS, Saipan, late December 1944

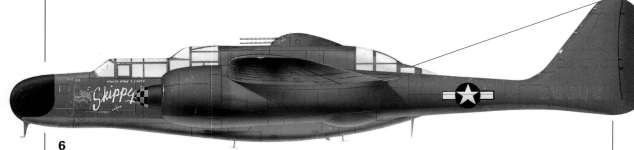

6
P-61A-1 42-5502 *"Skippy"*, crewed by 2Lt David Corts and R/O Lt Alexander Berg, 421st NFS, Tacloban Strip, Leyte, late 1944

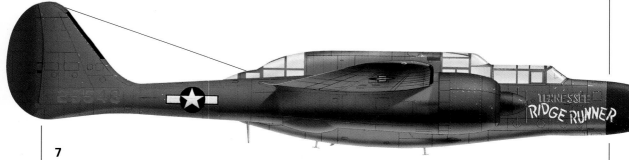

7
P-61A-5 42-5543 *TENNESSEE "RIDGE RUNNER"*, crewed by Lt John W Anderson and R/O Lt James W Mogan, 422nd NFS, Chateaudun, France, Autumn 1944

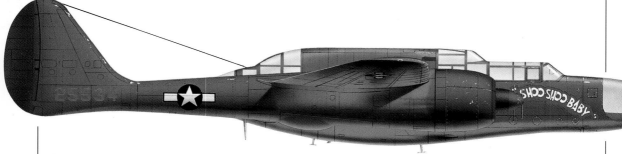

8
P-61A-5 42-5534 *"SHOO-SHOO-BABY"*, crewed by Lt Robert O Elmore and R/O Lt Leonard F Mapes, 422nd NFS, Chateaudun, France, Autumn 1944

9
P-61A-10 42-5598 *"SLEEPY TIME GAL" II*, crewed by Lt Ernest R Thomas and R/O 2Lt John P Acre, 6th NFS, Saipan, early 1945

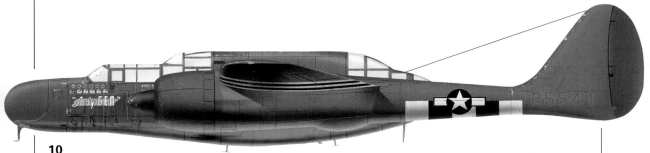

10
P-61A-5 42-5544 *"Lady GEN"*, crewed by Lt Paul A Smith and R/O Lt Robert Tierney, 422nd NFS, Florennes, Belgium, late December 1944

11
P-61B-6 42-39514 *HEL'N BACK*, 416th NFS, Horsching, Austria, June 1945

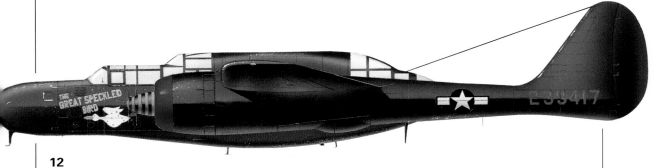

12
P-61B-1 42-39417 *THE GREAT SPECKLED BIRD*, crewed by Squadron Maintenance Officer Lt Dick Hoover and Senior Squadron R/O Lt Earl R Dickey, 416th NFS, Horsching, Austria, June 1945

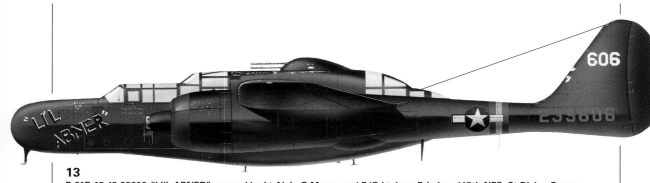

13
P-61B-15 42-39606 *"LI'L ABNER"*, crewed by Lt Alvin G Moore and R/O Lt Juan D Lujan, 415th NFS, St Dizier, France, March 1945

14
P-61A-10 42-5565 *"DOUBLE TROUBLE"*, crewed by 2Lt Robert G Bolinder and R/O Flt Off Robert F Graham, 422nd NFS, Etain, France, late 1944

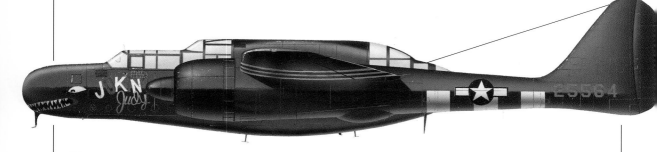

15
P-61A-5 42-5564 *JUKIN' Judy*, crewed by Lt Eugene Lee and R/O Lt Donald Doyle, 422nd NFS, Etain, France, late 1944

16
P-61B-6 42-39533 *Markey/HADE'S LADY*, 417th NFS, Giebelstadt and Braunschardt, Germany, June 1945

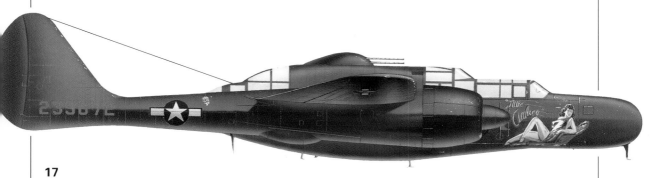

17
P-61B-15 42-39672 *"Little Audrey"*, 422nd NFS, Etain, France, late 1944

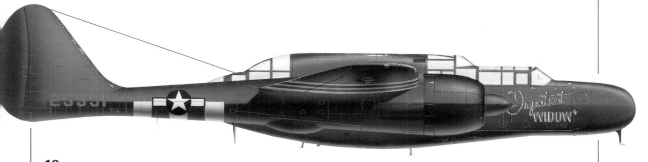

18
P-61A-10 42-5591 *"Impatient WIDOW"*, 422nd NFS, Etain, France, late 1944

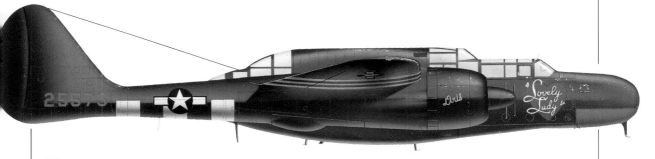

19
P-61A-10 42-5573 *"Lovely Lady"*, flown by Lt Donald Show, 422nd NFS, Etain, France, late 1944

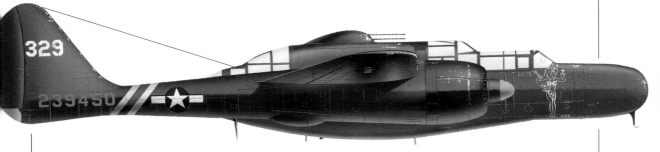

20
P-61B-1 42-39450, crewed by Lt Phil Hans, R/O Lt 'Doc' Holloway and Gunner Sgt Don Clancy, 419th NFS, Zamboanga, Mindanao Island, the Philippines, early 1945

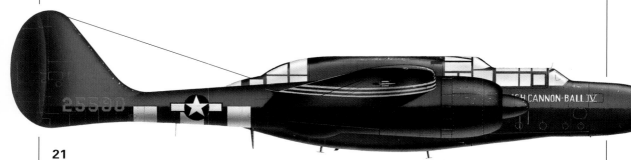

21
P-61A-10 42-5580 *WABASH CANNON-BALL IV*, crewed by Squadron Commanding Officer Lt Col Leon G 'Gilly' Lewis and Senior Squadron R/O Lt Karl W Soukikian, 425th NFS, Coloummiers, France, Autumn 1944

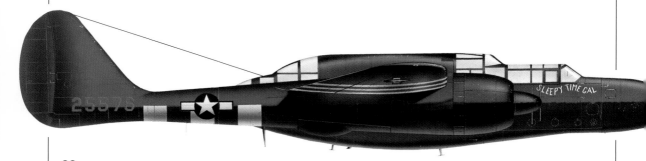

22
P-61A-10 42-5576 *SLEEPY TIME GAL*, 425th NFS, Coloummiers, France, Autumn 1944

23
P-61A-10 42-5569 *TABITHA*, crewed by Lt Bruce Heflin and R/O Flt Off William B Broach, 425th NFS, Vannes, France, October 1944

24
P-61A-10 42-5615 *"I'll get By"*, crewed by Capt John J Wilfong and R/O 2Lt Glenn E Ashley, 426th NFS, Kunming, China, November 1944

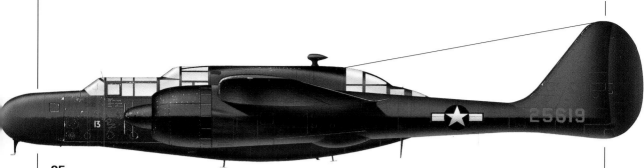

25
P-61A-10 42-5619 *SATAN 13,* crewed by Capt John Pemberton and R/O Flt Off C W Phillips, 426th NFS, Kunming, China, Autumn 1944

26
P-61A-10 42-5616 *Merry-Widow,* crewed by Capt Robert R Scott and R/O Flt Off Charles W Phillips, 426th NFS, Kunming, China, late October 1944

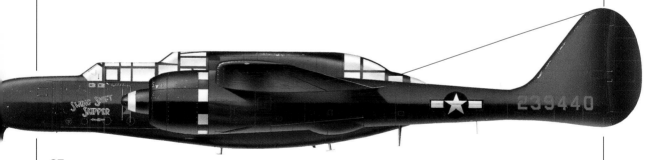

27
P-61B-1 42-39440 *Swing Shift Skipper,* crewed by 1Lt Arthur D Bourque and R/O 2Lt Bonnie B Rucks, 547th NFS, Lingayen, Luzon, the Philippines, February 1945

28
P-61A-10 42-39365 *Black-Jack,* flown by 1Lt Glen E Jackson, 426th NFS, Chengtu, China, late 1944

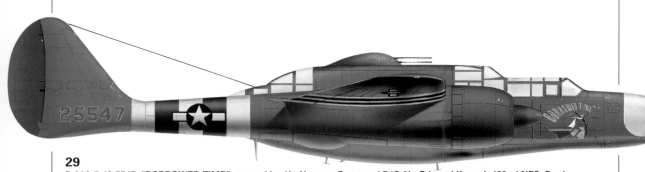

29
P-61A-5 42-5547 *"BORROWED TIME"*, crewed by 1Lt Herman Ernst and R/O 2Lt Edward Kopsel, 422nd NFS, Ford, England, July 1944

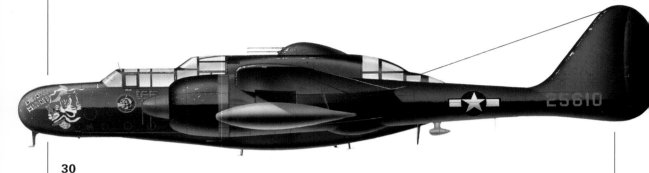

30
P-61A-11 42-5610 *MiDNiTE MADNESS*, crewed by Capt James W Bradford, R/O Lt Larry Lunt and Gunner M/Sgt Reno Sukow, 548th NFS, Iwo Jima, April 1945

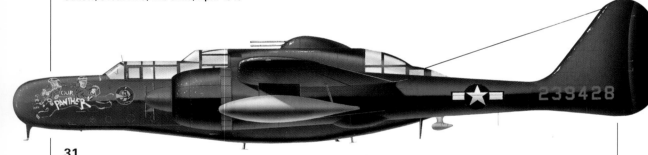

31
P-61B-2 42-39428 *OUR PANTHER*, crewed by 2Lt Fred M Kuykendall, R/O Flt Off Charles H Rouse and Gunner Cpl George Bancroft, 548th NFS, Ie Shima, Spring 1945

32
P-61B-2 42-39408 *Lady in the Dark*, crewed by Capt Sol Solomon and R/O Lt John Scheerer, 548th NFS, Iwo Jima, Spring 1945

33
P-61B-6 42-39525 *night TAKE-OFF*, 548th NFS, Iwo Jima, Spring 1945

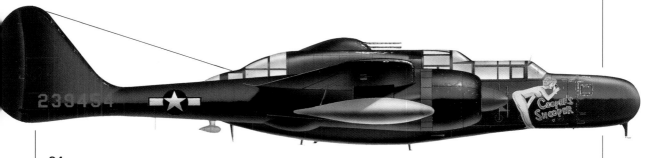

34
P-61B-2 42-39454 *Cooper's Snooper*, flown by 1Lt George C Cooper, 548th NFS, Iwo Jima, Spring 1945

35
P-61B-1 42-39405 *Victory Model/"ANONYMOUS" III/The SPOOK*, crewed by Lt Melvin Bode and R/O Lt Avery J Miller, 548th NFS, Iwo Jima, April 1945

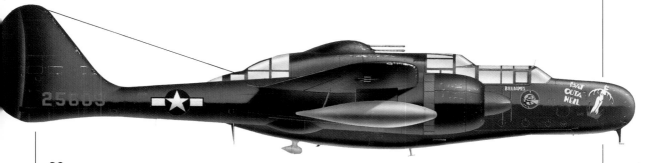

36
P-61A-11 42-5609 *BAT OUTA HELL*, crewed by Squadron Operations Officer Capt Bill Dames, R/O 2Lt E P D'Andrea and Gunner Sgt R C Ryder, 548th NFS, Kipapa Gulch, Hawaii, October 1944

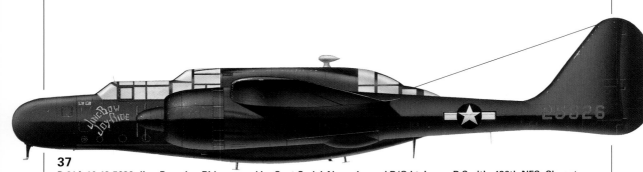

37
P-61A-10 42-5626 *Jing-Bow Joy-Ride*, crewed by Capt Carl J Absmeier and R/O Lt James R Smith, 426th NFS, Chengtu, China, February 1945

38
P-61B-6 42-39504 *MIDNIGHT MADONNA*, flown by both Lt Donald W Weichlein and Lt Frank L Williams, 549th NFS, Saipan, early 1945

39
P-61A-10 42-5623 *Sweatin' Wally*, flown by Capt Walter A Storck, 427th NFS, Myitkyina, Burma, late 1944

40
P-61B-6 42-39527 *BLIND DATE*, flown by Lt Milton Green, 549th NFS, Iwo Jima, early 1945

1
John W Myers, Northrop Chief
Test Pilot, Hawthorne, California,
1944-45

2
Lt John W Anderson (pilot), 422nd
NFS, Chateaudun, France, Autumn
1944

3
Lt Leonard F Mapes (radar observer),
422nd NFS, Chateaudun, France,
Autumn 1944

4
Lt Al Innerarity (radar observer),
425nd NFS, Vannes, France,
September 1944

5
2Lt Jean B Desclos (radar observer),
6th NFS, Saipan, late 1944

6
2Lt James Postlewaite (pilot),
422nd NFS, Maupertus (A-15), France,
July 1944

MEDITERRANEAN THEATRE

The P-61 failed to play a major part in the raging battles fought over North Africa and much of Italy, for both campaigns started well before the new Northrop fighter was ready for operational service. Lacking a quality American nightfighter, the USAAF turned to British-built Mosquitoes and Beaufighters to fill the role, both types having already proved themselves in-theatre with RAF units. Their resulting contributions to victory in the MTO were nothing short of outstanding, these aircraft being flown by units that had received intensive levels of training which later allowed them to successfully transition to the P-61.

The oldest night fighter organisation in the AAF was the 6th NFS, which was sent to the Pacific region following activation on 18 January 1943. The next four squadrons to form up (activated between 26 January and 17 February 1943) were all destined for the Mediterranean, the Twelfth Air Force controlling the assignments of the 414th, 415th, 416th and 417th NFSs. Although the Black Widow was still over a year away from achieving operational status, the need for nightfighter was immediate. The USAAF was faced with a dilemma, for it hadn't sufficient P-70s to equip frontline units, but it could at least commence the training process for nightfighter crews. British equipment would have to used in the interim until P-61s were available.

The 414th NFS would be the only one of the four units to have any type of impact on the war with the Northrop fighter. Having scored eight night kills in the Beaufighter, the squadron was fortunate enough to be the first unit in the MTO to receive the P-61, being issued with aircraft from 20 December 1944 onwards. The timing of their arrival was critical, for the 'Battle of the Bulge' had just commenced, and both Ninth Air Force

During the final days of the war many Luftwaffe bases that had not been completely destroyed were occupied by Allied squadrons. Here, a remarkably intact hangar at either Kassel or Braunschardt offers cover for 417th NFS groundcrewmen as they work on P-61B-6 42-39533 *Markey/HADE'S LADY* in June 1945 (*John Dowd*)

nightfighter units were having problems keeping their aircraft serviceable due to a shortage of spares. A combination of both factors saw the 414th send a detachment of P-61s from its base at Pontedera, in Italy, to Florennes, in Belgium, to work with the 422nd NFS. This was to be a tremendous stroke of good fortune for the 414th, for Twelfth Air Force records show that its units were credited with five kills flying the P-61, all of which were claimed by the 414th NFS's detachment in Belgium.

Capt Al Jones was one of the pilots sent to Belgium, and he summed up up his first impressions of the new fighter in the following quote;

'I felt that the new Black Widow was an extremely honest aircraft. It was very stable and made instrument flying quite easy. The low-speed handling qualities were excellent because of the spoilers used for lateral control, and it was also quite good in the high-speed regime. This wide range of performance was very desirable in night intruder missions, as the type of aircraft we intercepted ranged from speeds as low as 110 knots all the way up to 350 knots. The deadly armament of four 20 mm and four 50-cals allowed for a heavy concentration of firepower when strafing trains, trucks or other ground targets. Overall, it was very effective at the job it was designed to do!'

As the German offensive died down in late January 1945, the

The 415th NFS received its first P-61s in late March 1945, and within six weeks the war had ended. Squadron members Flt Off Norbert Konwinski (on the ground) and Lt P L Benoit pose alongside their Black Widow at Frankfurt just days after the German surrender (*Norbert Konwin*)

415th NFS pilot Lt Alvin Moore poses with his aircraft (P-61B-15 42-39606 *"LI'L ABNER"*) at St Dizier, in France, in late March 1945. His R/O was Lt Juan D Lujan (*Alvin Moore*)

Eighth and Ninth Air Forces prepared to resume their onslaught against Germany after the temporary setback of the 'Battle of the Bulge'. Allied daylight operations were overwhelming in February, with Germany being divided up into sections and each air force concentrating on targets within their assigned area.

During this month the 'Mighty Eighth' broke from its standard bombing procedures by allowing its 'heavies' to attack from altitudes of 10,000 ft or less, rather than the rigidly observed height of 25,000 ft. This change in ceiling also brought a change in mission composition, with units attacking in small flights rather than the previously standard large formations. The Eighth's fighters still escorted the bombers into Germany despite the relative lack of aerial opposition – pilots spent their time searching out strafing opportunities. The Luftwaffe had not posed a threat since Operation *Bodenplatte* on New Year's Day, when 800+ fighters had unsuccessfully attempted to destroy Allied aircraft at forward bases in a surprise dawn raid.

USAAF/RAF dominance of the air during the day meant that the Wehrmacht could only move safely at night, and although the P-61 units had every serviceable aircraft up and flying long intruder missions over enemy territory, they were too few in numbers to slow down the desperate efforts of the Germans. 414th pilot Capt Joe Jenkins was operating with his detachment out of Belgium at the time, and here he recalls a mission in February when the Germans were blatantly using trains to move equipment and supplies in the area of the Rhine and Cologne. He was flying his assigned P-61B-6 (42-39532), nicknamed *FIRST NIGHTER*;

'One of the missions that stands out in my mind, after all these years, was a night intruder type that took us over the Cologne area late one February night. It was a perfect night for the Germans to be on the move – no moon and a light ground haze. This worked well for us also in that the heavy ground fire that we had to face every night would be hampered somewhat! When we reached out target area, we immediately spotted a

The 414th NFS was the first MTO squadron to receive the Black Widow, and it was very successful with the fighter. Fortunately, the unit was able to participate in the 'Battle of the Bulge' in late December 1944, during which time it 'bagged' three of its five kills. Pilot Capt Al Jones (right) and his R/O 2Lt John Rudovsky actually enjoyed their successes after 'the Bulge' had been 'flattened out' when they downed a Me 410 and a Ju 88 during April 1945 (*Al Jones*)

Although the 417th NFS failed to score any kills with the P-61, it had already made its mark with the Beaufighter by downing nine enemy aircraft. *The Willing Widow* was operated by the unit from German soil during the final days of the war (*Claude Grappone*)

This line up shot was taken on 3 March 1945 following the delivery of the first P-61s issued to the 417th NFS to the unit's base at Lavallon, in France. The aircrafts' pristine all-black finish had been marred during post-shipping re-assembly by the removal of the protective tape from the airframe joints, leaving bare metal to show through where the paint had come away (*Richard McCray*)

locomotive that was pulling a long line of freight cars. I manoeuvred around to come in from the front and hit the engine first. This tactic was to get the train stopped. The initial pass worked, so we moved around and started working over the length of the train. We were able to destroy the engine and five cars. The ground fire was intense, though inaccurate.

'Later on in the mission, we pinpointed two more trains. More ammo shot up and one locomotive destroyed and one damaged. This time we had blown up 15 boxcars. There was a lot of ground movement all over the area. Suddenly, the RAF showed up with their heavy bombers and hit Cologne. We were right in close and they seemed to cover the entire area.

This triggered a lot of searchlights and ground fire. We flew more evasive action at that low altitude than at any other time I can remember. The RAF had stirred up a Hornet's nest! We were getting low on fuel and ammo by this time, so we headed back to our base.

'We were still combing the ground for possible targets though. As we were flying out of the area controlled by the Germans, we spotted two more trains. I made a quick circle of the area and dropped down on them. On a long firing pass, we ran out of ammo, with no noted results. We had no choice but to return to base. Although there had been no contacts made with night flying enemy aircraft, it had been a very busy night.'

The 415th NFS did not receive its first Black Widow at its St Dizier base until 20 March 1945, by which time the war was winding down and there was very little opportunity to intercept any enemy aircraft at night – the Germans were now critically short of fuel. Less than a month after

This evocative aerial view was taken over snow-covered German mountains soon after the 417th NFS had received its Black Widows. The squadron used coloured bands on the tail booms for identification (*John Dowd*)

P-61B-6 42-39514 *HEL'N BACK* was assigned to the 416th NFS in the summer of 1945. It is seen here up on jacks in an intact ex-Luftwaffe hanger at Horsching, in Austria (*Earl Dickey*)

The 416th either had a good artist in its ranks, or they took great pride in giving each aircraft a distinct personality, for all squadron aircraft wore nose art. P-61B-1 42-39417 *THE GREAT SPECKLED BIRD* was no exception, the aircraft being crewed by Squadron Maintenance Officer Lt Dick Hoover and Senior Squadron R/O Lt Earl R Dickey. This photo was taken at the squadron's Horsching base (*Earl Dickey*)

receiving the new aircraft, the 415th moved into Germany (Gross-Gerau) on 18 April, this base serving as the squadron's home until the end of the war. Air Corps records show that the unit was credited with 11 kills while flying the Beaufighter, but failed to register a single success with the P-61.

The 416th NFS was activated on 20 February 1943, its training period involving a stint at Orlando, which was at the time the centre for all night-fighter activities in the USA. They trained in the P-70, but when it came time to move to Europe, they were attached to the RAF within VIII

Crewed up and ready to taxy out for a night mission, this 414th NFS was operating from a base in Italy in the early spring of 1945 when this official USAAF photo was taken (*USAF*)

Capt Joe Jenkins flew P-61B-6 42-39531 *First Nighter* with the 414th NFS. A pilot with plenty of combat time on Beaufighters prior to be type rated on the P-61, Jenkins was part of the detachment that went to Belgium with the 422nd NFS. This photo was taken at the 414th base at Pontedera, in Italy (*Joe Jenkins*)

Fighter Command. In August 1943 they came under the guidance of the Twelfth Air Force and moved to the MTO. Crews quickly converted onto the Beaufighter, using the Bristol nightfighter to claim four kills before transitioning over to the Mosquito – they downed just one more enemy aircraft with the latter fighter. By the time the first P-61s appeared the war was over, the squadron being left to use the Northrop fighter for occupational duties only.

The final P-61 nightfighter squadron to operate under Twelfth Air Force control in the MTO was the 417th NFS, which was activated on the same day as the 416th. Like the latter unit, it too flew Beaufighters during a rather nomadic existence that saw the squadron fly from bases in Algeria, Corsica and France. The squadron got a lucky break in January 1945 when it was posted to Florennes, in Belgium, to work with the 422nd NFS as a result of the 'Battle of the Bulge'.

This deployment boosted their final total of kills to nine, all of which were scored with the Beaufighter, as they too did not receive P-61s until just before war's end. The 417th was based at Giebelstadt, in Germany, when their P-61s finally arrived, followed shortly thereafter by VE-Day.

The Black Widows that the squadron received were far from new aircraft, having had their top turrets and the 50 cal machine guns locked in the forward-firing position prior to their arrival. This meant that only pilots and R/Os would be flying, leaving gunners grounded yet again.

PACIFIC THEATRE

When the Allies were ready to launch the D-Day invasion, the area that needed to be 'swept clean' of enemy activity by the various friendly air forces was very small. Only two NFSs were assigned to handle the nocturnal chores, this modest force proving sufficient until the 'Battle of the Bulge'. Granted, if sufficient P-61s had been available then at least two more units could have been kept busy as a result of increased aerial activity by the enemy in the last months of the war. However, this was not to be, so they made do with what they had.

The vastness of the Pacific battlefield dictated a different approach, for two squadrons of P-61s would have achieved very little. Therefore, no less than eight squadrons of Black Widows were operating in the Pacific Theatre by war's end in August 1945. In order to further broaden their operational scope, some of these squadrons ran detachments that were scattered all over the forward combat areas, their primary responsibility being to protect high value assets such as airbases and aircraft from night marauding Japanese bombers.

The job of covering the night skies over an area many times larger than the ETO was split between three air forces, with the Fifth and Seventh Air Forces controlled three nightfighter squadrons apiece and the Thirteenth two. The breakdown was as follows:

P-61A-1 44-5527 *MOONHAPPY* of the 6th NFS was one of the most colourful Black Widows to see service in the Pacific, being crewed by R/O Lt Raymond Mooney (left) and pilot Lt Dale 'Hap' Haberman – the third member of the team was Gunner Pvt Pat Farelly. The aircraft's name was derived from the surnames of Mooney and Haberman, this crew/aircraft combination finishing the war with four kills (*Dale Haberman*)

Fifth Air Force	Seventh Air Force	Thirteenth Air Force
418th NFS	6th NFS	419th NFS
421st NFS	548th NFS	550th NFS
547th NFS	549th NFS	

These squadrons received their full complement of Black Widows over a period of seven months.

Following the successful American landings on Guadalcanal in August 1942, it became painfully obvious that the new invading force needed the services of nightfighters, for the Japanese launched their most brutal night attacks of the entire Pacific campaign. The first USAAF nightfighters finally reached the area in February 1943 when a detachment ('Det B') of the 6th NFS arrived with their 'stop-gap' P-70s (A-20 light bombers that had been hastily converted into nightfighters). The 'new' fighter's limitations were numerous, however, and the high flying Japanese Mitsubishi

G4M 'Betty' bombers simply operated at ceilings greater than the P-70's altitude range, thus rendering it next to useless.

The situation was so critical that the 6th NFS also made limited use of P-38s and P-40s during their early days in-theatre.

The need for an effective night-fighter grew as Allied forces took the fight to the Japanese on an ever broadening front across the Pacific rim. This requirement became so great that the 6th NFS was forced to send another detachment ('Det A') to fly P-70s over New Guinea, where they provided some mod-

R/O Lt Charles Ward and pilot Lt Robert L Ferguson stand by their famous P-61A-5 42-5554 *THE VIRGIN WIDOW* prior to flying a night mission during the defence of Saipan in late 1944. This 6th NFS Black Widow was photographed by just about every member of the squadron (*Ernest Thomas*)

During the early summer of 1945, Iwo Jima was transformed from a quiet Pacific island into a well-developed 'superbase'. Visible in the original print of this aerial view are P-61s lined up alongside the runway, seen in the upper centre of the photograph. These belonged to the 549th NFS, and parked below them to the right are a large number of long-range P-51 Mustangs. Mt Suribachi can be seen at the extreme bottom right of this shot (*Bill Charlesworth*)

549th NFS pilot Lt Bill Charlesworth (right) poses with the rest of his crew at their Iwo Jima base in May 1945. P-61B *Hop'N Ditty* was Charlesworth's assigned aircraft, the squadron having received their first Black Widows in October 1944 (*Bill Charlesworth*)

Early-morning ground fog over Iwo Jima often proved to be more dangerous to P-61 crews than the enemy, reducing visibility over the airfield to zero. This P-61 was one of four 548th NFS aircraft caught by the weather one morning whilst returning from their nightly patrol. Although the first nightfighter – P-61A-11 42-5610 *MiDNiGHT MADNESS*, flown by Capt James Bradford – made it down safely (it blew a tyre), the pilot of the second aircraft (P-61B-1 42-39405 *Victory Model/ "ANONYMOUS" III/The SPOOK* seen here), Lt Melvin Bode, came in blind wide of the runway. When he tried to adjust his approach his aircraft clipped the ground, bounced off the top of the recently-landed P-61 (resting starboard wing low in the background, and duly struck off charge without having been repaired) and slid on its belly until finally coming to a halt, its 20 mm cannon firing as it went – the aircraft was subsequently declared a write-off. The third aircrew baled out off the coast and the fourth had sufficient fuel to stay aloft until the fog had lifted (*Mel Bode*)

icum of night protection. At this time, the arrival of the P-61 was still almost a year away, with the first examples to arrive in the Pacific being assigned to the 6th NFS on 1 May 1944.

All the USAAF's original nightfighter squadrons were equipped with the P-70 during their early combat tours, units such as the 6th, 418th, 419th and 421st NFSs also using whatever other types they could get their hands on to help bolster their numbers. Aircraft which fell into the latter category included the P-38, P-40 and even the B-25, all of which were used to 'buy time' for vulnerable Allied bases under the threat of attack by creating a barrier that would slow down the Japanese intruders.

Of these assorted types, the B-25H was easily the least qualified for nightfighting, although this did not seem to deter its primary operator in this role, the 418th NFS. This unit was the only nightfighter outfit present at the newly-built airfield on Watke Island, which had essentially been converted into one huge USAAF base. It housed the 90th Bomb

Group (BG) with its B-24 Liberators and the P-47 Thunderbolt-equipped 348th Fighter Group (FG), both of which were high value assets deemed vulnerable to Japanese night attacks. In response, the 418th kept their converted bombers airborne throughout the night. When the unit was finally relieved of its duties on 18 August 1943, the crews flew their Mitchells back to Hollandia to begin the long and tedious training period leading up to their transition to the P-61.

All Black Widows that were destined for the Pacific had to go through the depot in Hawaii, the first batch of Northrop fighters to be processed being early A-models fitted with top turrets. The first units

548th NFS crew chief Sgt Reed Stockwell relaxes after getting Capt Bill Dames's P-61 *BAT OUTA HELL* ready for another mission from Ie Shima in 1945. This Black Widow was the second '*BAT* to serve with the unit, the first having been lost some months earlier (*Reed Stockwell*)

to receive these aircraft were the 6th and 419th NFSs, both squadrons being specially chosen because of their frontline experience. Only two days separated the arrival of the first P-61s to both units, the 6th getting their first aircraft on 1 May 1944, followed by the 419th on the 3rd.

It took a while for the squadrons to get up to speed with the new fighter, both units feeling their way during numerous practice missions. After several weeks of training, P-61 crews were declared operational, and the 6th NFS drew first blood with the Northrop fighter on 20 June, followed some time later by the 419th on 5 August.

With the first units up and running, things rapidly sped up in respect to introducing the P-61 into wider frontline service. The most rapid transition onto the fighter was performed by the 421st NFS, which received its premier 'Widow on 1 June and achieved its first kill on 7 July.

2Lt Carl H Bjorum was a pilot within the 421st NFS, and here he recalls one of his early missions in the P-61 (his R/O was 2Lt Robert C Williams whilst his assigned gunner was S/Sgt Henry E Bobo);

'The first time I fired the guns in a Black Widow, I was shooting at a Japanese bomber at night, with all the confidence in the world! My total time in the aircraft was 44 hours and 20 minutes! This was a good indication of the ease of transition and the straight forward nature of the aircraft.

'Our GCI told me to take a heading of 210° and to climb up to 18,000 ft. They were picking up two different enemy aircraft in our area. When we reached our "perch", we could see small flashes of AA fire and four large flashes that were probably

Lt Dale Haberman is seen at the controls of P-61A-1 44-5527 *MOONHAPPY* off the coast of Saipan in late 1944. The nose art displayed on his P-61A was later replaced with more elaborate artwork (*Dale Haberman*)

Sgt Don Clancy served as a gunner aboard the 419th NFS's *Uncle Sugar Able* on Noemfoor Island in 1944/45 – he is seen here in late July 1945. The unit's Detachment 'A' flew P-61s from this base between 25 July and 27 November 1944, the 419th having received its first Black Widows on 3 May 1944 (*Don Clancy*)

P-61A-1 42-5524 *"Midnight Mickey'"* was amongst the batch of early-production aircraft delivered to the 6th NFS in the olive drab scheme. The team of pilot 2Lt Myrle McCumber, R/O Flt Off Daniel Hinz and Gunner Pvt Peter Dutkanicz shot down two 'Betty' bombers in this aircraft – note the freshly painted kill symbol immediately beneath the cockpit (*Daniel Hinz*)

bombs being dropped by the Japanese intruder. I was told to orbit north of Japen Island until the "bogey" emerged from all that AA fire. Through VHF communications, I heard another of our fighters that was also up radio that he was closing in on one of the enemy bombers. I was told to break off because the pursuit was coming into my sector.

'Seconds later, we spotted tracers spewing out into the darkness, these were followed by a ball of fire which dove toward the water and burst on impact. It had been a confirmed kill! Now, the business at hand . . . there was still another Jap bomber in the area. I was vectored onto a heading of 80° with an immediate turn to 220°. At that time, Williams got the "bogey" on radar at a range of five miles and slightly above us. As we got closer, the scope became "clouded", which meant that the bomber was dropping "window" – foil strips dropped to confuse opposing radar scopes. He was still visible on the scope, so we continued to close right through the Jap's defensive ploys.

'Both Bobo and I obtained a visual at the same time. The target was at 1500 ft and I confirmed it was a "Dinah" Type 100. It was in the process of making a gentle starboard turn. He was lined up perfectly and the gunner gave him a quick burst with the .50 cals. The "Dinah" levelled out and I fired a three-second burst from my 20 mm, which was joined by a stream of rounds from the top turret. Numerous hits. The "Dinah" went into a steep diving turn to port, and I kept on his tail in an almost vertical dive. The airspeed was up to 400 mph and we were about 600 ft behind. We fought the "Gs" and pulled out at 5000 ft, vaulting back up to 10,000 ft.

'Seconds later, we observed a flash of light in the distance and we presumed it was our "Dinah" exploding. The other Black Widow ("Asphalt 16") that had made the previous kill confirmed that they had seen an enemy aircraft explode and fall out of the sky along the shoreline of Japen Island. The wreckage was confirmed the next day by a patrol in the area. We had expended 200 rounds of 20 mm and 1000 rounds of .50 cal.'

For some reason this kill was never entered into the record books, although Bjorum and Williams would go on to score two confirmed kills. This action had taken place on the night of 7 July 1944.

The aircraft ('Asphalt 16') operating in the sector alongside Bjorum was flown by 421st crew Capt Owen Wolfe (pilot) and R/O 1Lt Byron Allain. They would end their tour with the unit as its top scoring team, with four confirmed kills – they flew a P-61 named *'Dame de la Nuit'*.

A handful of kills scored by the Black Widow were actually achieved without a shot having ever been fired, P-61 crews chasing enemy aircraft at such low altitudes over the water that they crashed into the Pacific. Perhaps the most unique P-61 kill of them all though fell to 421st NFS crew

Some of the most elaborate nose art to come out the Pacific theatre was produced at Kipapa Gulch and on Saipan, 6th NFS aircraft P-61A-1 44-5526 *NIGHTIE MISSION* being a prime example (*George Irwin*)

The 38th Service Squadron was kept busy on Guadalcanal preparing new aircraft that had arrived from the USA by ship in crates. This unit assembled P-61s for use by all squadrons in-theatre, the aircraft seen in this photo being destined for the 419th NFS, which was operating on the 'Canal at the time (*USAF*)

Lt David Corts and his R/O Lt Alexander Berg when ten Japanese aircraft raided their base on Owi Island at night. As usual, the USAAF airfield was protected by four P-61s working regular zones around the island, and when GCI picked up the inbound bandits, the closest crew – pilot Lts Corts and Berg (flying their assigned P-61A-1, 42-5502 *"Skippy"*) – was duly alerted. They were vectored in behind one of the Japanese bombers, and as Corts was getting close enough to fire, Berg yelled out that his rear cockpit has been lit up by incoming tracers. The pilot immediately broke off to get out of the line of fire, although the Japanese bomber closing up behind the P-61 continued to fire, duly hitting the aircraft that Corts had been after just seconds before. It burst into flames and crashed into the ocean. It had been a unique kill, and Corts was given full credit without having fired a shot.

The crews from the surviving 'Betty' bombers 'put out the word' that there was a new weapon lurking in the dark skies over Owi Island. Gone was the P-70 and night-flying P-38, both of these makeshift types having been replaced by a purpose-built aircraft that could match anything the Japanese had both for speed and performance at altitude. To make matters even worse for the Japanese, this new weapon could 'see in the dark'!

The 6th NFS in particular quickly exploited the P-61 to its fullest potential, and by war's end its crews had achieved 16 confirmed kills, put the unit in second place among all American nightfighter squadrons. The 6th's leading team comprised pilot 1Lt Dale Haberman and R/O 2Lt Raymond P Mooney, who would finish with four confirmed victories in colourfully-decorated P-61A-1 44-5527 *MOONHAPPY*.

Despite all this eventual success, the P-61 was initially plagued by its fair share of mechanical and technical 'bugs', as Capt Ernest R Thomas, 6th NFS pilot of P-61A *SLEEPY TIME GAL*, recalls;

'We were operating from Saipan at the time. One night we were up and our GCI vectored us toward an intruder, which was south of our base. One thing we had learned quickly was that the gunsight on the Black Widow did not work real well

at night. This was emphasised on this mission in which we made our first of two kills. When I brought my gunsight to bear on the enemy aircraft, the complete circle reticle hid the target! I fired a burst and when nothing happened, I dropped the sight to find the target. I brought the sight back on target and was able to destroy it with the second burst. As soon as we were able, we had the top half of our gunsights painted out to allow us to see the target, while still having the dot and lower half of the reticle visible. This worked satisfactorily and was the type of sight we used when we went over to Iwo Jima to work with the new 548th NFS.'

Capt Thomas achieved his second score in *SLEEPY TIME GAL* whilst operating with the 548th NFS;

'We made AI contact on this "bogey" at a distance of seven miles. Since altitude reports by ground radar were not always reliable, I had developed a technique of helping my R/O "search" for his initial contact by raising and lowering the nose of the aircraft. This provided a larger "search" area until initial contact could be made. We began closing while the "bogey" was flying a slow, climbing, course heading south of Iwo Jima. He had apparently missed the island and he was flying too slow for us to obtain a visual before overshooting him. My Gunner, Cpl Jessie Tew was able to get a positive i.d. with binoculars, proving it to be a "Betty". We continued to make closing passes, overshooting, and then making another 360° turn to pick up our contact and close again and again!

'This went on for about 45 minutes all the while the "bogey" continued climbing and heading south. We were at the limits of our range, but were given permission to pursue a little longer. It wasn't long before the Jap pilot levelled off and we moved up quickly behind him. At 600 ft, I made a visual on him by looking out of the corner of my eyes. My R/O called out the distances – 600-400-200 ft. All of a sudden, he started making a turn to the left. I didn't know if I had been seen or the pilot had realised he had missed "Iwo". I pulled to the right, then turned back into him, pulling the sight through his right engine, and firing a quick burst of all guns as I passed directly under the plane, almost ramming him as I went by. The one burst proved to be enough, as his engine was on fire.

The crew chief of 421st NFS P-61A-1 42-5502 *"Skippy"* makes some last-minute adjustments to his charge prior to it flying another mission from Tacloban Strip, on Leyte. This unit ended the war with 13 enemy aircraft destroyed (*USAF*)

The 6th NFS's groundcrews were extremely proud of the unit's combat record, as this decorated maintenance trailer shows – 12 of the 16 kills scored by the squadron are detailed on it in decal form. The aircraft which provides the backdrop for this photograph is undergoing routine maintenance on its radar unit (*Vance Austin*)

'This would be a spectacular kill in a few seconds. The bright light caused by the fire forced me to go back on instruments in order to orient myself. I had barely focused on the instrument panel when the entire sky lit up from a tremendous explosion which startled me into thinking it was my own ship. My R/O told me the enemy bomber had blown up into three sections. This was, presumably, from exploding fuel and the load of bombs he still had on board. As the pieces fell into the cloud cover below, there was another large explosion. There was no doubt that we had made the "kill"!'

The aircrew of *MOONHAPPY* prepare to climb aboard their illuminated P-61 at the start of yet another night patrol off the coast of Saipan. The R/O was positioned in the extreme rear of the crew nacelle, separating him from the gunner and pilot (*USAF*)

Far removed from the factory shots of the P-61's interior seen in chapter one, this view shows the well-used cockpit of P-61A-10 42-5598 *"SLEEPY TIME GAL" II* of the 6th NFS. The photo was taken by the aircraft's pilot, Lt Ernest Thomas, and also reveals such details as his parachute and leather helmet, respectively draped over the seat and control yoke

As the Black Widow pilots continued to make minor adjustments to their equipment, their Japanese opponents began to realise just how effective the Northrop fighter was. Indeed, those bomber crews lucky enough to have survived an encounter with the P-61 with their aircraft still intact undoubtedly briefed their colleagues once they had returned to base on just how devastatingly accurate the new American nightfighter was!

The P-61s flown by the 6th NFS were A-models fitted with both sets of guns which, at first, were loaded with tracer rounds to help improve shooting accuracy. This fitment was swiftly dropped, however, when it was discovered that the tracers often alerted previously unwitting enemy pilots to the presence of a nightfighter. The quartet of 20 mm cannon were loaded with a deadly mix of armour-piercing, incendiary and high explosive rounds, which could swiftly inflict mortal damage to an enemy aircraft with a just a handful of hits.

As previously mentioned, the 418th NFS gave up their unique B-25H 'nightfighters' for P-61s in early September 1944, their commanding officer at this time, Maj Carroll C 'Snuffy' Smith, being well-known for his expertise in the art of nightfighting. He would finish the war as the highest ranking American nocturnal ace in World War 2, having downed five aircraft in a P-61 and two while flying a 'stop-gap' P-38 rigged with searchlights!

Four of his Black Widow kills were achieved in the same night – half during the evening of 29 December 1944 and half during the early morning hours of the 30th. In the following quote, Smith recalls that long night when he and his R/O, Lt Philip Porter, wrote them-

Lt Milton C Green's P-61B-6 42-39527 *Blind Date* is seen parked on Saipan in late February 1945. At this time, the 549th NFS was waiting for the Marines to secure Iwo Jima so that they could 'set up shop' on the island (*Milton Green*)

'Iwo's' South Field was jammed with 549th NFS Black Widows from 20 March 1945 until war's end. Volcanic ash and dust played havoc with squadron aircraft based on the island, as this shot clearly shows. In this view, P-61B-6 42-39504 *MIDNIGHT MADONNA* has had its canopy area covered over with a tarpaulin (*Milton Green*)

A beaming groundcrewman 'fondles' the stunning nose art painted on *MOONHAPPY*. All the original olive drab P-61A-1s issued exclusively to the 6th NFS were painted with superb nose art (*Vance Austin*)

selves into the record books flying their famous P-61, *'Time's-A-Wastin'*;

'It was a moonless night, with broken clouds around 5000 ft. Our job was to provide protection for a convoy of ships that was making its way to Manila Bay. The first attempt to penetrate our barrier was done by a twin-engined Japanese bomber known as an "Irving". Porter vectored me straight in on him and we got a visual from behind. My position was perfect, so I squeezed off a couple of short bursts and the bomber dropped like a rock, completely engulfed in flames. This provided great entertainment for the troops on the ships below us.

'I guess we were in the right place at the right time, because shortly after that first kill, we made contact with another intruder coming into our area. He took no evasive action and we locked him up quickly, just like the first kill. A quick burst or two sent him down in flames. What a night! The rest of our patrol was uneventful, and we headed back to base to take on more fuel. We would launch again to work the same area in the early morning hours of the 30th. We didn't take on more ammo because we had shot down two aircraft already, and the chances of having more opportunities before dawn were very slim!

'We took off again and were briefly into our shift when we picked up another bandit. Porter located him (on radar) at three miles out. I was told to drop down to 500 ft, and that began one of the damnest chases I had ever witnessed . . . almost at sea level. Most of this time was spent with flaps down for slow speed work. I was beginning to doubt what my R/O was seeing on the screen. Suddenly, I saw the "bogey" and it was a "Rufe" (floatplane fighter based on the A6M Zero) about 300 ft away. I quickly lined him up and fired a short burst with my 20 mm. The "Rufe" exploded and hit the water. My concentration at that low altitude had been so intense that the kill seemed to take only a few seconds.'

Although Smith was now nearing the end of his second mission for the night, having achieved a trio of kills, his scoring run wasn't over yet;

'Evidently, the Japanese were well aware of the movement of a convoy in the vicinity because there had been a lot of activity over our patrol area. Forty-five minutes after the "Rufe" hit the water, Porter picked up yet another blip on the screen. We had him at six miles and 5000 ft. By this time it was 0700 hours, and due to the light from the rising sun, I was able to see him pretty far out. This time I figured we had our hands full – it was a Japanese fighter, known as a "Frank" (Nakajima Ki 84), and the first one I had ever seen. This aircraft was similar to our P-47, and it would not be an easy kill. We had two things going against us – the lack of complete

P-61B-2 42-39408 *Lady in the Dark* has been well publicised over the years because of its stunning nose art, the 548th NFS machine being flown from bases on both Iwo Jima and Saipan. There is a possibility that this aircraft made the last aerial kill of World War 2, although this claim has never been officially recognised (*Ed Jones*)

Parked in the background with its engines idling, P-61B-1 42-39405 *Victory Model/"ANONYMOUS" III/The SPOOK* is quickly checked over by its crew chief following the completion of minor maintenance work on Ie Shima in the the early summer of 1945. Pilot 1Lt Mel Bode and R/O Lt Avery Miller were assigned to this aircraft (*Mel Bode*)

darkness, and I was not sure how much ammo we had left because we did not reload during our pit stop.

'I felt that I had a few rounds left, but with the morning light, I had no place to hide if I made the "Frank" mad. I stayed below and closed to 75 ft. We were dangerously close, and every detail of the fighter was clear. This was an unusual position for a P-61 pilot to be in. I let him have a burst of 20 mm. The results were awesome! This was my first chance to see what multiple 20 mm cannon hits could do to an aircraft! It was a memorable sight. The "Frank" simply disintegrated and the pieces fell into the sea as I frantically tried to avoid the debris.

'It was 0707 hours and we headed back to base. The first thing I did when we landed was check my ammo. To mine and Porter's surprise, we had only expended 382 rounds for four enemy aircraft! We had 200 rounds left – I will always remember that night!'

Following the 418th's receipt of P-61s in September, the 547th and 548th accepted examples in October and duly saw combat in areas quite distant from one another. The 547th would be a key player in the battles fought to regain the Philippines, operating from Owi Island, Tacloban, Leyte, Mindora and Lingayen, on Luzon. In order to effectively cover such a large area, they had several detachments scattered away from these primary sites. By war's end the unit had destroyed six enemy aircraft, with their first kill in the P-61 coming on 25 December 1944.

The 548th NFS commenced its work-ups with the Black Widow at the same time as the 547th, this colourful unit perhaps being best known for the elaborate nose art painted onto their new fighters. Their primary duties included the air defence of Saipan, Iwo Jima and Ie Shima, which saw them patrolling the main B-29 bomber route between Saipan/Guam and Japan. By this stage of the war the 547th and 548th NFSs found hostile 'trade' hard to come by due to the diminishing number of operable Japanese airfields, although the latter squadron was still able to claim five confirmed kills by VJ-Day.

The primary target for the P-61 in the Pacific was Mitsubishi's G4M 'Betty' bomber, which had been able to bomb American bases after dark with almost total impunity prior to the introduction of the Northrop fighter. The latter's P-70 predecessor would be 'hanging on its props' and still be unable to reach the 'Bettys', and although the searchlight-equipped P-38s that

P-61A-1 44-5528 "Jap Batty" was yet another of the dull drab olive early model aircraft delivered to the 6th NFS. Its crew, pilot 1Lt Francis C Eaton, R/O 2Lt James E Ketchum and Gunner S/Sgt William Anderson, knocked down two 'Betty' bombers in this aircraft. Ketchum is seen on the far right in this shot, with Eaton stood next to him (*USAF*)

548th NFS pilot Capt James W Bradford shows off the freshly-applied artwork on the nose of P-61A *MiDNiTE MADNESS*. This aircraft was the first Black Widow so dubbed, and it was eventually destroyed in a landing accident caused by ground fog on Iwo Jima on 20 April 1945 (*James W Bradford*)

The legend of *Midnite Madness* was kept alive with a replacement aircraft, which was adorned with an identical nose art and the numeral 'II' beneath the name. The original crew also remained together, and they are seen here with their regular groundcrew – kneeling to left is pilot Capt Bradford, to his left is R/O Lt Larry Lunt and standing in the middle is Gunner, M/Sgt Reno Sukow (*James W Bradford*)

had been hastily produced 'in the field' enjoyed some success, it proved unable to halt the night attacks. By late 1942 new versions of the 'Betty' fitted with supercharged engines were reaching the front, these bombers being capable of speeds in excess of 300 mph and even higher ceilings.

Unlike previous types, the Black Widow was able to reach any altitude that the Japanese aircraft might be lurking at, which came as a nasty surprise for the navy crews – indeed, on many occasions USAAF pilots reported that their targets continued to fly straight and level, with no evading tactics performed, even after radar detection.

548th NFS personnel Capt James W Bradford, R/O Lt Larry Lunt and Gunner Sgt Reno Sukow experienced this one night when they caught a 'Betty' trying to penetrate the air defences around Ie Shima. As usual, they were flying their regular P-61A-11 42-5610 *MiDNiTE MADNESS*. Capt Bradford remembers the mission;

'It was expected to be a routine patrol with very little chance of spotting any enemy activity. We were airborne off of Ie Shima at 1835 hours. There was still plenty of light when we took off. The first two hours were uneventful, then at 2110 hours our GCI notified us that they had a blip at 20,000 ft, 30 miles out, coming our way. We had been cruising at 9000 ft, so I eased us up to 23,500 ft to give us an altitude advantage when we picked up the intruder on our AI.

'We continued to close in on the "bogey". At a range of eight miles, we locked on and our closure speed gave us at least a 30 mph advantage. Lt Lunt brought us right in to a distance of 7000 ft, where Sgt Sukow made a positive identification with the aid of his night binoculars. The moon was bright, and there was no doubt we had a "Betty" bomber in our sights! My guess is that the Japanese pilot was not aware we were behind him, because there was no evasive action, and his airspeed remained constant.

'I eased *MiDNiTE MADNESS* to within 700 ft of the "Betty". My gunsight bracketed the aircraft as I eased off a quick three-second burst. No effect. I know the "Betty" took a lot of hits, but it continued to fly straight and level. I repeated with another five-second burst, which set his port engine on fire. To make sure, I squeezed off a third volley and it amplified the fire which rapidly spread to the "Betty's" fuselage. It was an unusual sight because the light from the fire lit up this huge rising sun that was painted on the side of the bomber. By this time the "Betty" had started a turn to the left and a gradual descent. The pilot seemed to have control until the bomber went into a steep dive.

'We followed it down to a dangerously low altitude as the enemy aircraft hit the water and exploded. At that moment, Lt Lunt commented that he might have another "bogey" on the screen – it was "window" that had been put out by the "Betty" right before it exploded. Up until that time, no "window" had been used. At the end of the shoot-down, we were at an altitude of 1500 ft. The rest of the patrol was uneventful'

With the number of aircraft contacts rapidly dwindling, units like the 547th NFS started to find other missions for the fighter. Squadron pilot Lt Francis J Raidt was a great supporter of the Black Widow in its intruder role, as the following interview given by him to V Fighter Command shows:

'The defensive role of nightfighters in the SWPA has been reduced by Allied air superiority. We just are not getting much night activity from the Japanese.

The gunners in the 6th NFS held a dual role, for they not only loaded the guns but fired them as well. Facing the camera is Sgt Jerry K Lucas, whilst squadron artist Sgt Leroy Miozzi, wearing the painted jacket, has his back to the camera. Both veterans of numerous missions over the Pacific, they are seen here loading 20 mm rounds into the belly magazine of a squadron Black Widow (*USAF*)

'We have one of the best aircraft ever made for the dual role. Due to the effectiveness of day fighters, the enemy has been forced to conduct their operations during the hours of darkness! With certain modifications to our aircraft, we can add to our defensive mission with one that will make us a deadly force in the offensive night intruder role. With the added ordnance capability (bombs, napalm and rockets) and our ability to execute precision night flying, the results could be very impressive!

'The value of this can be shown by example. Recently, a P-61 was given the assignment of bombing Tuguegarao airstrip. Two American single-engine fighters had arrived in the area at dusk from a base outside of Luzon. They would recon the target area right before dark. The objective was changed at the last minute, however. The P-61 was contacted in the air on its way to the target by an advanced radio station. Under its direction, the primary target was changed to a target at Aparri, where a Japanese general, his staff, 400 troops and stores of ammunition were located.

'The Black Widow flew to Aparri and placed a direct hit on the target (which was still burning 14 hours later)! The intruder then strafed the airstrip, where a twin-engine bomber and two fighters were staging. Next was a secondary target at Tuguegarao, which was attacked at low-level. The result were unobserved, but there were no attacks on friendly installations that next night. I might add that this mission was flown on a moonless night and in weather that required three hours of instrument flying! This is a new facet of the P-61's potential, and it is here to stay!'

Although aerial targets were now rarely encountered, the 6th NFS enjoyed a 'purple patch' during the final six weeks of 1944 whilst ranging out on long patrols from its base on Saipan. Encountering an abundance of targets, the unit downed nine aircraft between 25 December 1944 and 2 January 1945, all bar one of these being 'Betty' bombers. One of these kills fell to Lt Robert L Ferguson, R/O Lt Charles Ward and Gunner Sgt Leroy F Miozzi in P-61A-5 42-5554 *THE VIRGIN WIDOW* on the night of 26 December, which turned out to be one of the busiest nights of the war for the 6th NFS – it seemed that the Japanese were sending every 'Betty' in-theatre to hit Saipan. Lt Ferguson recalls that night;

'We were scrambled at 2200 hours. We were talking with our GCI as we lifted off. They had an intruder on the scope coming in fast at 20,000 ft. At that time it was 40 miles out. We got in behind and started closing. The "bogey" was descending, so I slowed to about 120 mph in order not to overshoot. Ward said that wasn't good enough, so I dropped full flaps. I was told to make a hard 360° turn and lose as much altitude as possible.

Conditions got so overcrowded at Lingayen, on Luzon, that the 547th NFS's dispersal stretched down virtually onto the beach. Note the piles of scrap and used parts left behind by past tenants dumped between the surf and the parked aircraft. The squadron operated from this base between 16 January 1945 and war's end (*Paul Diehl*)

A new P-61 is reassembled after having been uncrated at Hickam Field, in Hawaii. All early Black Widows destined for the 6th and 419th NFSs were prepared at this site prior to heading to the front. Later in the war, a number of new aircraft were shipped to Guadalcanal (*USAF*)

We lost about 6000 ft in the turn. That still wasn't good enough, so we did another 360° turn, losing about the same altitude as before. This "Betty" had dropped down on the deck, so I initiated a third turn, coming out at 1500 ft!

'I was concerned that we might be trying to intercept a boat, and could therefore hit the water. Down this low, our radar screen was getting cluttered up, so we lost the "Betty". According to my R/O, the enemy aircraft was still well below us! After this pursuit, we were sent after two more, which turned out to be just about as frustrating. A short time later, we were up on our "perch" when GCI informed us of another intruder coming our way. This time it was 45 miles out and changing altitude frequently. We dropped down to 15,000 ft and had to climb back up to 17,000 to stay level with the "bogey". Ward picked him up at five miles.

'We were encountering a problem that was common to the P-61 – our overtake speed was 40 mph, and we were close to overshooting. I lowered the flaps and my airspeed dropped 50 mph. Now he was pulling away from us. Retracting flaps, we shot forward and were 1200 ft to his rear and level. We continued to close down to 300 ft, where I was able to get a

visual. It was a "Betty". Directly behind and level with the target, I let go with a burst that hit his port engine and fuselage. There was a small explosion inside the fuselage, followed by a red glow. The aircrew in the "Betty" had a problem . . . a fire inside the aircraft!

'We were dangerously close, and if the bomber had exploded, we would have been in trouble. I throttled back and moved off to the right side. We were flying off the bomber's wing. I continued to slow down in an effort to get behind and fire another burst. The "Betty" continued to lose airspeed and its nose

The war is just days from being over, and a lone 418th NFS crew chief works on his Black Widow soon after the unit had moved to Okinawa in late July 1945. Following VJ-Day, the squadron remained on the island and changed its designation to the 4th All Weather Squadron (*Royce Gordon*)

This 547th NFS crew (from left to right, Col R L Johnson, an observer from Wing HQ, pilot Lt Ken M Schreiber, R/O Lt Bonnie Rucks and Crew Chief, T/Sgt John C Crough) caught a Japanese 'Tess' in the landing pattern at its base in the Cagayen Valley and shot it down. Schreiber and Rucks were on a night intruder mission at the time (*Roy Oakes*)

550th NFS crew of *"Ohlami"* pose by their Black Widow on Zamboanga in early summer 1945. Pilot Lt Newell Witte is at the extreme left, and next to him is R/O Lt H C O'Brien. They named the aircraft by taking the first two letters from the three states the crewmen were from – Ohio, Louisiana and Michigan (*Newell Witte*)

Pilot Maj Victor G Modena (wearing the sombrero) poses with other members of his 550th NFS crew in front of his assigned P-61, *The Gay-Blade*. With very few enemy aircraft in the air by this late stage of the war, the squadron flew numerous night intruder missions from bases at Sanga Sanga and Puerto Princesa (*George Freed*)

dropped down in a gentle descent. By this time the aircraft was burning furiously from the waist to the tail. The nose dropped even more and it went into the ocean, exploding on impact. We returned to base at midnight, where we learned that we had expended a total of 100 rounds of 20 mm – *THE VIRGIN WIDOW* was a virgin no more! My gunner, Leroy Miozzi, was the artist that had painted the artwork on our fighter. He painted lines through the *'VIRGIN'* and drew a ring on her finger!'

Not all scrambles resulted in kills, and although most crews were left frustrated, they all responded to an emergency call to take-off with great vigour. Unknown to them, their efforts often caused enemy crews to turn back, or jettison their bombs prematurely.

Sgt Jerry K Lucas, a gunner with the 6th, recalls the final days of December when there was a flurry of enemy activity around Saipan. His memories of this time illustrate just how serious aircrews took the call to scramble, and why time to take-off was so important;

'There was one night that stands out over the others. It was 26 December 1944. I was in the armament shack that night when I got the word that my crew had been ordered to scramble. My Chief rushed me out to the end of the runway in a truck that was parked nearby. When I arrived at the aircraft, my pilot, Lt Bill Robbennolt, and R/O, Lt Richard Phillips, were already rolling. They had already checked the mags. By the time I climbed up the ladder and pulled the lowered door closed behind me, Robbennolt was bolting down the runway at full throttle – time was critical. If I had arrived 30 seconds later, they would have left without me.

'Airborne, GCI gave us a vector of 090° to 20,000 ft. We headed north of the island. The inbound intruder was at 16,000 ft and orbiting. For some reason or another we lost contact. We tried to find him but to no avail. Another enemy intruder was detected by GCI, and we were told it was 10,000 ft below us at a distance of 20 miles. We went after it, but before we could get an AI lock, the GCI lost it. They didn't show any other enemy aircraft on their scope so we flew back to our base. The scramble had lasted 50 minutes and produced no results.'

The 418th was also experiencing substantial activity by Japanese floatplanes at around this time too. Pilot Lt Bertram C Tompkins was heavily involved in the action, and

2Lt James W Schuler and his R/O Flt Off Arthur D Miller take a look at the new 310 gal tanks that have been recently attached to the pylons of their P-61. The 550th NFS began using the stores to fly long-range night intruder missions, the tanks weighing in at around 2000 lbs apiece when full (*Newell Witte*)

here he relates some of the enemy tactics used against the P-61s during attempted interceptions;

'While we were operating out of Morotai Island, the enemy used methods to counteract us. They used "window" a lot, and it proved to be very effective at first. It jammed the GCI scope much more that it did the AI on our ships. The tactics that they used with the "window" was to drop it when they entered GCI range, and then they would exit the same way, hoping that the GCI set was jammed.

'They also frequently used floatplanes. They would come in range first and draw us out. While we were following them, their bombers would come in and make their bomb runs without any interference. In the meantime, the "floats" would land on water, wait for a period of time, and then go back to their base, flying very low so GCI would not pick them up. We were certain that the Japs had GCI on the tip of Halmahera Island and so directed their bombers over the target, keeping them out of range of our P-61s.'

Lt Tompkins's R/O, Lt Vincent Wertin, recalls one such encounter;

'One night on local patrol, we were vectored in on an intruder. I took over when I registered contact at a distance of seven miles, and guided Tompkins in to a distance of 3000 ft. From that point, he could see the exhaust flames, and at 2000 ft, the single exhaust pattern turned into two! We thought we had a twin-engine bomber. We increased speed because the enemy aircraft looked like he was farther away than that. We came in very fast and at 500 ft, Tompkins discovered that it was a Jap "float". Realising that he could not slow down soon enough, we made a tight 360° turn and went in again. This time we dropped some flaps and closed much slower. Calling off the distances, we narrowed it down to 800 ft. At that time, we shot off a long burst.

Maj Robert A Tyler, the commanding officer of the 550th NFS (the final nightfighter squadron to be formed in World War 2), poses at a forward base in the Pacific on 1 August 1945 (*Robert Tyler*)

The "float" disintegrated, crashing into the water.'

This mission was flown on the night of 9 December 1944, and the team of Tompkins and Wertin would finish the war with three kills to their credit – two of them against Ki 61 'Tony' fighters.

The final two nightfighter squadrons formed during the war

6th NFS crew R/O Flt Off Richard Phillips (left), pilot 2Lt Wilfred C.Robbennolt (centre) and Gunner Sgt Jerry K Lucas were photographed in front of the *The Virgin Widow* while out on the flightline. This trio flew many night intercepts in a number of different aircraft (*Jerry Lucas*)

With its three-digit number visible on the nosewheel well door, this P-61B is easily identified as belonging to the 419th NFS. The tail code on this new Black Widow was 42-39450, and it was one of only a handful of P-61s that carried nose art other than a name on the forward crew nacelle (*Don Clancy*)

The crew assigned to *Trigger Happy* comprised (from left to right) R/O Lt Fred O Paige III, pilot Lt E M Tigner and Gunner T/Sgt Abraham Lincoln Stein. The latter individual was one of the most highly decorated members of the 549th NFS, having served in the Pacific since early 1941! This photograph was taken on Iwo Jima in the early summer of 1945 (*E M Tigner*)

were the 549th and 550th NFSs, The former being activated on 1 May 1944 and the latter following suit 30 days later. Following training and full equipment with Black Widows, the 549th began its journey to the frontline from Kipapa Gulch, Hawaii, after which the unit spent a month on Saipan. Their primary base of operations would be on Iwo Jima, and they 'set up shop' there just as the island was being rid of the last vestiges of Japanese occupation.

The 550th began its combat tour in December 1944 in New Guinea, although it did not receive its first P-61s until 6 January 1945. Unlike the 549th, the unit was given the task of covering a large operational area, and it was forced to send detachments to such bases as Middelburg Island, Tacloban, Zamboanga, Sanga Sanga and Puerto Princesa. By the time both squadrons became operational, few aerial targets were to be found (only the 549th would draw blood in the night skies, claiming a single kill), so they specialised in night interdiction and intruder missions instead. The 550th, in particular, became very proficient in this tasking, working with air-to-ground rockets, bombs and napalm.

As the invasion of the Philippines proceeded, the 550th established their stronghold at Tacloban, on Leyte, being given the primary mission of defending US assets in that area. This tasking included routine defensive patrols, protective cover for Allied equipment on land or water and strafing designated targets. From Tacloban, they covered all of Leyte, Cebu, Panay, Negros, Bohol and Mindanao.

550th pilot, Lt Robert G Graham, participated in numerous sorties with the unit during the Spring of 1945;

'I can remember one mission we flew over to the island of Negros. We had just received some replacement pilots, and one of them was scheduled to fly my wing. This would turn out to be one of the nastiest strafing missions I had ever been on. The new pilot was Lt Don Coski. He asked if I had any advice for him before we took off, and I replied that the lower and faster you flew on this type of mission, the safer you were.

'Our assignment was to fly predawn cover for the ships and invasion forces. When it got light, the infantry would radio us and tell us what was giving them the most trouble, and we would then go down on

the deck and strafe it. Dawn broke and we learned that the Japanese troops were retreating up into the mountains. They had established some gun positions there and were effectively working over the friendly troops. Our assignment was to take out these guns. I radioed to Coski to follow me. These guns were in a position that was designed to give us hell. The steepness of the mountains forced us to turn around at the end of our strafing runs and go back out the same way we came in!

'On our first run, I had all my guns firing and the Japanese were throwing everything up at us. Suddenly, Coski came on the radio and yelled he had been hit. I asked him if the aircraft would still fly and he said "yes". When we ran the gauntlet back out, and I told him to fly over to a small strip on Panay that our forces had just captured and wait for me. I went back to the targets and expended the rest of my 20 mm ammo. When I landed, Coski was up on the wing of his airplane trying to dig a tree limb out of the leading edge. It had to be seven or eight inches in diameter! It was one heck of a souvenir of his first combat mission, and a tribute to the ruggedness of the P-61!'

R/O Flt Off Seymour Bylsma and pilot Lt Robert G Graham have suited up prior to climbing aboard their 550th NFS P-61 (named *Helen*). Both men flew several daytime sorties in support of army troops fighting to retake the Philippines (*Robert Graham*)

MiDNiTE MiSS/'My Pet' **is shown between sorties on Saipan, this 548th NFS Black Widow surviving the war unscathed. Like many other war-surplus P-61s from this squadron, the aircraft was flown to Clark Air Base, in the Philippines, soon after VJ-Day and eventually scrapped in 1948 (*Walt Wernsing*)**

The crew of P-61A-11 42-5609 *BAT OUTA HELL* – R/O 2Lt Eugene P D'Andrea and pilot Capt William H Dames – study their mission assignment prior to take-off. The latter individual was the Squadron Operations Officer for the 548th NFS. Dames was later killed in the mid-1950s in a B-47 crash in the mid-west (*Mel Bode*)

6th NFS crew R/O 2Lt Jean B Desclos, pilot 1Lt James C Crumley and Gunner Pvt Otis O'Hair pose for a USAAF photographer with their flight gear on (*Jerome Hansen*)

548th NFS pilot Capt Bill Dames is seen sans his flying apparel with the original *Bat Outa Hell* – P-61A-11 42-5609 (*Bill Gates*)

Freshly-painted P-61A-11 42-5609 *BAT OUTA HELL* of the 548th NFS is seen in flight over its base at Kipapa Gulch, in Hawaii, just before the unit departed for Saipan (*Bill Dames*)

The 549th was the only squadron to operate all of its aircraft from a single location, finding enough action locally to keep all its crews occupied. Iwo Jima remained a 'hot spot' for several months after the US Marines had seized the island, the unit finally arriving on 'Iwo' from Saipan on 20 March 1945 after the airfield had at last been deemed safe.

A large percentage of the 549th's missions consisted of long-distance patrols over water, many of which involved lengthy and frustrating interceptions that resulted in little reward for the crews concerned. Nevertheless, the squadron succeeded in keeping most Japanese bombers away from the island, the enemy often exiting the area faster than it had arrived. As a result, P-61 crews rarely got within firing distance of a 'bogey', leaving the 549th to score just one confirmed kill.

Squadron R/O, Flt Off George W Hayden, recalls the details of just such a sortie that he was involved in;

'On 1 June 1945, my pilot, 2Lt William Sill, and I had a running dogfight with a Japanese intruder that lasted for over two hours and took us a third of the distance to Japan, from Iwo Jima. We intercepted this aircraft about 40 miles out. As we closed the gap, I saw several flashes down on the water – the bomber had jettisoned its bomb load, and they had exploded as they hit the water.

'This intruder was leaving the area at full speed. They were using "window" and other radar jamming techniques. One of them caused heavy snow on the scope, which made it difficult to pick out their blip. The other type caused many criss-crossed, 45° angle, dotted lines on my screen. I believe it was called "grid jamming". They usually used this when we got within 3000 ft. At this distance, they started hard evasive action. They learned quickly that they could not out-turn us. They did make use of their best trait – high altitude.

'They would usually sit up at 34,000 ft while we were topped out at under 30,000 ft. All we could do was look up at their vapour trails that seemed brilliant in the moonlight. On this night they were all over the place, and believe me they knew exactly where we were at all times. Twice we got to within 600 ft before they would initiate evasive action. At one point, we were closing on them at 18,000 ft when we both went through a heavy cloud layer. Our luck didn't change here because the cloud interior was filled with freezing moisture. When we emerged, our wings were iced up and we were flying sloppy. It took a few minutes to get the ice off and continue the pursuit . . . which was moving closer to Japan!

'We never did get close enough to even get a positive i.d. on this guy. I know for a fact that the 548th had tangled with an aircraft with similar results. They had reported that the aircraft they were after had never let them get close enough to identify, and at times it did slow rolls and

Lt Fred Kuykendall's P-61B-2 42-39428 *OUR PANTHER* on Ie Shima in the late spring of 1945. The remaining members of this 548th NFS crew were R/O Lt Charles H. Rouse and Gunner Cpl George Bancroft (*Joe Weathers*)

Sgt Harold Burdue is seen with *Nocturnal Nuisance,* this P-61 being flown by the 421st NFS. The photo was taken on Noemfoor Island in August 1944 (*Harold Burdue*)

549th NFS P-61B-6 42-39504 *MIDNIGHT MADONNA* was regularly flown by two different pilots, namely Lt Donald W Weichlein and Lt Frank L Williams. The aircraft is seen on Iwo Jima in the spring of 1945 (*Don Weichlein*)

other manoeuvres as they tried to get within firing range. I have always believed it was a very sophisticated Jap aircraft that went by the Allied code name of 'Myrt' (Nakajima C6N Saiun). It was equipped with all types of radar. It knew where we were at all times.'

During the P-61's brief service life in the Pacific, its operators were mentioned many times over the airwaves by the infamous Japanese propaganda broadcaster 'Tokyo Rose'. It was common knowledge amongst Allied troops that if she singled out any particular unit on the radio, it meant that they were doing their job! Lt Robert Graham recalls one such broadcast, and how it could have led to disaster;

'At the time, our 550th detachment had responsibility for protection of Morotai. We had three aircraft here, and we were being relieved by the Australians and their Spitfires. Needless to say, the Japanese knew every move we made.

'The first night that the Aussies had the duty, the Japs came over in force and bombed the heck out of us. They got one of the ammo dumps. "Tokyo Rose" came on the air and stated, 'How did you boys on Morotai like that? You're going to get it again tonight'. We knew the Japs liked to come over between 10pm and midnight, so we told the Aussies to let us have it for tonight. We were up and ready when we heard GCI say they had an unidentified aircraft on the screen. When they told us "unidentified", that meant it had no IFF (identification friend or foe) working.

'We tracked the target and got right up behind it. All I had to do was shoot. GCI came on the air and yelled, "Don't shoot. That is a friendly fighter!" It proved to be one of the Aussie Spitfires that was up, and his timing could have been fatal! All of the Allied aircraft were equipped with IFF, but this Spit had one that didn't work.'

Lt Graham finished his combat tour with the 550th having flown 53 missions, which amounted to 175+ hours of combat time.

Both the 549th and 550th remained active in the Pacific after hostilities ceased, the latter unit finally being inactivated on 1 January 1946, followed by the 549th on 5 February.

The Black Widow quickly disappeared from the USAAF/USAF inventory postwar, being replaced in the All-Weather Interception role by the North American F-82 Twin Mustang in 1947-48. With the air force rapidly moving towards an all-jet force as the 1940s came to a close, the life of the F-82 was also to be short-lived, for the F-89 and F-94 were soon ushered into service as 'the new kids on the block'.

CHINA/BURMA/ INDIA THEATRE

Aside from its sterling work in the Pacific, the Black Widow was also called on to perform nocturnal patrol duties over another huge land mass in the form of the China/Burma/India (CBI) front – indeed, between China and Burma alone, the area of operations amounted to more than 4,000,000 square miles. The CBI was also 'home' to more than one million Japanese troops. The responsibility for the nocturnal air defence of vast tracts of the Allied frontline fell to just two USAAF nightfighter squadrons, namely the 426th and 427th NFSs. In an effort to 'spread' their services as far as possible, both units would keep numerous detachments scattered out over a very large area in an effort to deter Japanese night intruders. When the war ended the 426th would be credited with five kills, whilst the 427th failed to register a single aerial victory, thus reflecting its air-to-ground mission.

The two squadrons formed just 30 days apart, and remained close to each other throughout their training cycles. Initially, they were meant to be assigned to different theatres, the 426th heading for India and the 427th scheduled to be sent to the Mediterranean, and then to the USSR on a special assignment.

The 426th was duly despatched to CBI in early August 1944, receiving its first P-61s on the 25th of the following month while still based close to Madhaiganj, in India. The unit then moved into China on 5 October, setting up its centre of operations at Chengtu in order to support a myriad of detachments – the 426th's headquarters would remain at Chengtu until 15 March 1945.

The 427th NFS, meanwhile, had had its Soviet move vetoed by the communists, thus leaving the squadron with its aircraft in Egypt. The

Two members of the 426th NFS pose in front of P-61A-10 42-5619 *SATAN 13*, with Capt John Pemberton sat in the cockpit. This shot was taken at one of the unit's forward bases in China (*George Bushaw*)

Black Jack has been secured for the day, its cockpit being protected against the dust by a tarpaulin. Swirling sand storms were commonplace at the far-flung forward bases that the 426th operated out of. The assigned crew for this P-61A was 1Lt Glen E Jackson (pilot) and R/O 1Lt Frank N Moran (*Glen Jackson*)

Close-up shot of Capt John Wilfong's P-61A-10 42-5615 *"I'll get By"* just after he had shot down a Japanese bomber on the night of 21 November 1944 – the crew chief featured in this photo remains unidentified (*John Wilfong*)

unit subsequently moved to Pomigliano, in Italy, on 3 September 1944, having by now become familiar with the intricacies of the P-61. By this late stage in the war, southern European skies had been all but swept clear of Axis aircraft by the four USAAF nightfighter squadrons already in-theatre, so the 427th NFS, led by Lt Col James S Michael, was posted instead to Barrackpore, in India. However, this site proved unsuitable as an operational base due to its primary role as a major assembly centre for aircraft being shipped into theatre – the new P-61s arriving for the 426th all came through this airfield. By the end of October, the 427th had moved to Pandaveswar, again in India, which put it in a much better position strategically to deploy detachments into Burma and China.

Returning to the 426th, this unit had been rushed into China in order to relieve the much-needed 311th FG P-51Bs of bomber airfield protection duties. The latter group had initially been given this task because of the more frugal fuel requirements of its Mustangs in comparison with the P-47s which had previously filled the role. Fuel was a precious commodity in China due to the difficulty of transporting it over the Himalayan mountain range – indeed, the bulk of the gasoline which made it across the 'Hump' was consumed by 'gas-guzzling' B-29s.

At the time of the exchange, the 426th was several aircraft short of its full complement, so it was decided to give them eight of the 427th's P-61s. This decision was not popular with members of the latter unit.

After waiting around to regain its full complement of aircraft, the 427th was finally ready to form up and move to its new main base at Myitkyina, in Burma, in late 1944. Further delays of a technical nature

The 426th NFS's top scoring nightfighter team pose by their mount, P-61A-10 42-5626 *Jing-Bow Joy-Ride*, which shows both of their kills. On the left is R/O 2Lt James R Smith and to the right pilot Capt Carl J Absmeier. The pair downed two 'Lily' bombers in three days (*Carl Absmeier*)

had also delayed the unit at Pandaveswar when the squadron's engineering and communications people had had to complete extensive modifications to the new fighter to make it reliable in the field. The two most time-consuming jobs involved installing radio compasses and changing all tail surfaces – it seems that although the latter had been spray-doped at the factory, the harsh weather conditions found in the CBI revealed that it was better if they were brush doped. This procedure would insure a longer performance life for the surfaces.

These technical problems aside, the gasoline shortage almost saw the 427th stripped of its P-61s when it was felt that there was no need for two nightfighter squadrons in-theatre. Fearing the worst, Lt Col Michael even got permission for his pilots to be checked out in the P-47 Thunderbolt

A brand new P-61 is unloaded, uncrated and prepared for service (with either the 426th or 427th) at an assembly centre in India. Note that the ADF antenna has not yet been installed on top of the crew nacelle (*Garry Pape*)

Capt Walter A Storck smiles for the camera whilst sat in his personal mount, P-61A-10 42-5623 *Sweatin' Wally*. Storck was one of the original 427th pilots to go through training with the newly-formed unit at Hammer Field, California (*Fred Blanton*)

Letting down over a mountain range into a valley, two 426th NFS P-61s near their forward base as they return from an orientation flight. The Black Widow crews would work the rivers and roads at night, looking for truck and troop movement (*Albert Gann*)

in order to provide a margin of survivability for his squadron in the day fighter-bomber role should his P-61s be grounded. Fortunately, the 427th NFS did not have to give up its beloved Black Widows.

Shortly after the B-29s began successfully raiding Japanese targets, their bases were declared a top priority target for the enemy's night intruder force. After two such raids had been carried out (on the nights of 8/9 and 26/27 September 1944), Gen Curtis LeMay finally demanded the services of a night-fighter squadron, and on the eve of 6 October (the very night the Japanese had scheduled their third major raid), a detachment of P-61s from the 426th NFS arrived at Chengtu. By the night's end, the enemy knew that their raids would not go unnoticed, although the Japanese had no choice but to continue sporadic attacks until the final assault on 19 December. During a total of 10 raids only 43 aircraft were encountered, resulting in very little damage being caused.

Although few aircraft were physically located by the P-61 crews during the raids against the B-29 bases, there was nevertheless a considerable amount of enemy activity tracked by Allied radar at night. This put the 426th detachments at Kunming and Hsian in an enviable position. For example, on the night of 29 October, Capt Robert R Scott and his R/O Charles W Phillips (flying their P-61A-10 42-5616 *MERRY-WIDOW*) intercepted a lone Kawasaki Ki-48 'Lily' bomber that was inbound into their patrol sector at 11,000 ft. Their GCI picked up the intruder at a dis-

tance of 40 miles out, and Scott pushed the throttle fully forward and closed as fast as he could.

Receiving two vectors during the closure, he was steadily climbing from his 5000-ft 'perch' up to the level of the enemy bomber. They locked on at three miles and moved on in, undetected, to 1000 ft, where a positive i.d. was made. At this point the 'Lily' was making a slight climb with an airspeed of only 120 mph. At a range of 500 ft, Scott opened fire just as the enemy pilot began violent evasive action with a hard, deep, diving turn to port. The action then turned into a dogfight that lasted five minutes, with the Japanese pilot trying everything he could do to shake his stalker.

Col Winston W Kratz (right) congratulates Capt Robert R Scott after the latter had scored the 426th NFS's first kill whilst flying P-61A-10 42-5616 *Merry-Widow*. Col Kratz was considered to be the 'Godfather' of the American nightfighter programme, having been involved in recruiting the original cadre of crews (*L C Reynolds*)

Once down at an altitude of 4000 ft, the P-61 pilot was again in a position to fire. At a high speed and in a diving attitude, Scott fired another burst of 20 mm, the rounds hitting all over the target's starboard wing and engine. Flaming fragments blew off of the bomber, and flames flashed out from the underside of the right engine. Realising he was too close, and that the aircraft could explode, Scott pulled hard right and climbed – his altitude had deteriorated down to 3000 ft. The 'Lily' never pulled out, exploding on impact. Upon returning to base, the crew discovered that one of the prop blades on their P-61 had a deep nick in it from a piece of flying debris. This had been the 426th's first confirmed kill.

Three weeks later Capt John J Wilfong and his R/O, Lt Glenn E Ashley, were launched on a routine patrol in their assigned P-61A-10 42-5615 *'I'll get By'*. Here, mission details are recalled by Capt Wilfong;

'After taking off, we came under GCI control, who promptly vectored us on to an enemy aircraft which was flying at 6000 ft. Due to our fast closure speed, we overshot the target and lost him. Minutes later we were again directed onto another aircraft at the same altitude. The heading was 270°. GCI brought me to within four miles, at which time Lt Ashley picked the "bogey" up on his radar screen. While closing in, the enemy aircraft started taking evasive action, initiating a rapid climb up to 14,000 ft. We continued to close the gap, and with the bright moonlight, we were able to get a positive i.d. at 600 ft. It was a Japanese "Dinah" (Mitsubishi Ki-46). From a position of 5° above and 5° to starboard, I gave it a quick burst with my 20 mms (this would probably have been about 40 rounds). No sooner than I had quit firing, the "Dinah" exploded in front of us. It was a textbook intercept!'

The 'Dinah' was Japan's staple twin-engine reconnaissance aircraft, being was one of the fastest (in excess of 375 mph) machines flown by either side in the CBI. Although its speed and ability to reach 35,000 ft challenged anything the USAAF could range against it, neither attribute was of any use for nocturnal reconnaissance. Crews were therefore forced to slow down and fly at a much lower altitude in order to achieve their

Capt John J Wilfong (on the left) and his R/O, Lt Glenn Ashley, celebrate their 'kill' following a long night mission over China. This crew participated in the P-61 delivery flight over the Himalayan Mountains which saw the 426th finally move into China (*Bob Brendel*)

Day orientation flights were regularly flown from forward bases in China, this shot probably being taken at Ankang or Liangshan by the second of two Black Widows making a pass over the airstrip at the completion of just such a sortie. Another 426th P-61 can be seen waiting to take-off (*Joe Greenbaum*)

Armourers have pulled the 20 mm cannon from *Jing-Bow Joy-Ride* so as to facilitate cleaning and minor maintenance work. Regular servicing of these weapons was crucial in the poorly-equipped forward areas for the 20 mm cannon was the only internal armament carried by the 426th NFS's Black Widows (*Carl Absmeier*)

purpose, thus making them easy prey for the Black Widow. Aside from photo-recce work, modified 'Dinahs' also performed fighter-bomber missions in China.

Although the Japanese were fully aware of the P-61's entry into service in the CBI, and knew only too well of its effectiveness, many bomber crews felt secure in the knowledge that there were too few Northrop fighters in-theatre to cover the entire front. The enemy's intelligence on just how few Black Widows were in the CBI astounded even the USAAF, as the following incident reveals.

One of the 426th NFS's distant detachments had a P-61 crew standing alert when it was ordered to get airborne for an intercept. Whilst taxiing out, the landing gear lock was accidentally released, collapsing the left main gear – the aircraft bent a prop and slightly damaged the left tail boom. The next day, during her radio broadcast, 'Tokyo Rose' mentioned this incident, and the fact that the detachment only had two P-61s left in flying condition! Her source of information was never detected.

The terrain in China was so rugged that it caused permanent echoes on the ground controllers' radar screens (some mountains took up over half of the screen), and this made picking out enemy aircraft very difficult. . The Japanese had already figured this out from previous experience in-theatre, and so started to fly most of their nuisance raids right down on the deck. It was impossible for the P-61's radar to pick up any aircraft at distance without the help of GCI, so freelance interceptions by the 426th and 427th were almost impossible.

As the number of Japanese nuisance raids decreased, it became difficult to justify the nightfighter's defensive role. Much wear and tear was being experienced by the versatile P-61 whilst performing just one role, so orders arrived from Fourteenth Air Force HQ that gave the

426th permission to participate in night intruder missions. These would all be carried out from forward bases at Hsian, Ankang and Liangshan, with the primary missions being to disrupt enemy troop movements and their hours of rest. With the change of roles, squadron aircraft received modified bomb racks – the combination of bombs and 20 mm cannon allowed the unit to inflict considerable damage on most targets.

One of the P-61s involved in these missions was P-61A-10 42-39365 *Black Jack*, and its assigned pilot, 1Lt Glen Jackson, recalls the early intruder work;

'From Ankang, our missions saw us night strafing and bombing anything we could find in the valley that was beyond the 10,000-ft mountain range east of our base. We would ease across the mountains, drop down and start hunting. The most numerous targets were truck convoys, bridges, trains and troop bivouac areas. The latter were easy to spot because of the small charcoal fires that they cooked by.

'Our favourite external load was a combination of napalm, general purpose (GP) bombs, para-frag clusters and anti-personnel bombs. When a convoy of trucks was spotted, the ideal situation was to strafe and disable the lead truck. This blocked the entire column. With them having to drive with no lights, when we did stop the lead truck, there were usually several accidents caused as they ran into one another. This made it easy for us to make several passes with our 20 mm cannon. There were many incidents where we had to make strafing passes down narrow canyons. Once our napalm had lit everything up, we realised just how narrow those gaps were. Sometimes, the Japanese would use mortars with timed fuses, against us. They would fire as we came overhead and the mortar rounds would burst with a bright flash. It was scary but not effective.'

The 427th was outfitted with rocket tubes for 4.5-in projectiles by mid-February, thus completing the trio of new weapons (bombs and napalm being the others) available for ground attack work. Factor in the aircraft's 20 mm cannon, and the end result was the most lethal fighter-bomber in-theatre.

427th NFS P-61A-10 42-5633 *Betty Jean* **is shown here staging out of a forward base (probably Chengkung) in early 1945. Some of the unit's forward detachments were so small that they comprised just two aircraft (*Ed Best*)**

Towards the end of the war many P-61 squadrons made effective use of the aircraft in the night intruder role, fitting bombs, rockets and napalm under the wings. This 427th aircraft displays its newly-rigged rocket tubes and bomb shackles (*Dan Hagen*)

Myitkyina was a major staging base in Burma for the 427th NFS, this shot, taken in late 1944, showing most of the squadron's complement of aircraft. Also note the B-25s parked to the left of the P-61s (*Glenn Holcomb*)

An anonymous 427th NFS pilot gives the thumbs up before taking off on another night intruder mission. The half-moon symbols on the fuselage indicate regular patrol missions, whilst the ones at the bottom with a lightning bolt through them show the number of armed night intruder missions flown against ground targets (*Don Loegering*)

By the 27 March 1945, the squadron was well their new role with a sweep over a network of roads south of Lashio. During four nights of intruder missions, one P-61 alone flew seven sorties, dropping 2000 pounds of bombs, firing 26 rockets and expending 1825 rounds of 20 mm. Two weeks later, HQ Tenth Air Force gave the 427th permission to begin day and night offensive reconnaissance.

The success of this new mission led to some 427th NFS crews in forward areas starting to fly daytime intruder sorties with P-51 escorts. These sorties served a dual purpose for they allowed crews to become familiar with the terrain, and thus be more effective in the same areas at night.

Both squadrons were now getting the maximum use out of their aircraft in all roles, records for the 426th, for example, showing that in a one month period they dropped 156 100-lb bombs and fired over 5000 rounds of 20 mm.

One of the unit's pilots at this time was Lt Gerald Stein, who recalls one of these missions, flown with his R/O, Flt Off James F Rogers;

'We were flying out of Hsian for an early hour, low-level mission. This night, we would be monitoring enemy rail activity. We took off at about 2am, flew up the Yellow River to the first railroad and set a northerly course, following the tracks for about 90 miles. We were taking sporadic hits from small arms fire, when suddenly one round hit us in one of the gun compartments, exploding one of our 20 mm rounds. There was no visible damage, so we continued on.

'Twenty miles further, I observed welding repairs being done on a previously damaged railroad bridge. We banked around and made a strafing pass with no visible results. We were so low that we almost took the cab off of a repair truck. Our flight to the north continued until our fuel level got low enough for us to head back in the opposite direction. Forty miles back down the track produced some headlights that indicated a train was coming. My approach brought us back around and my firing pass was set up from the right rear. I wasn't sure where my 20 mm rounds were converging, but I could see sparks flying along the tracks, so I walked them right on up and through the engine. We were using armour-piercing rounds. As we passed over, Rogers reported a plume of steam spouting from the engine, so I guess we stopped it.

'By now the fuel was critical, and we headed back to base. As we were about to land, I noticed that the left engine cylinder head temperature was extremely high, and after landing we discovered damage to the fins on one of the lower cylinder barrels – a .25 cal round had also holed the right drop tank, along with further small arms holes in several places. It had been a successful mission for us, but it would not have been if we had had a liquid-cooled engine instead of radials!'

As the early months of summer rolled around, the pounding of the Japanese homeland increased. By this stage in the war the Imperial Navy had been completely devastated, leaving troops on the China front short of both reinforcements and supplies. This allowed the Allies to starve the still substantial enemy force into surrender, physically weakened Japanese troops suffering a series of defeats at the hands of the Chinese Army in particular.

When the war finally ended, the 426th was ordered to return all of its detachments to Kunming, and on 18 September squadron personnel loaded into transports for the flight back to India. After a long sea voyage home, they arrived back at Camp Kilmer, where the squadron was officially inactivated on 5 November 1945.

The 427th, meanwhile, had accomplished something that very few squadrons had been able to do during the war – it had participated in four theatres, namely Italy, north Burma, China and central Burma. The unit shipped out ahead of the 426th, and by 29 October 1945 it been inactivated.

During their brief existence, both units had covered a greater land expanse that any other nightfighter squadrons during World War 2. They had successfully protected the major airbases in-theatre despite operating in some of the worst conditions experienced in the CBI, managing to shoot down a handful of Japanese aircraft in the process. Both units had also made a significant contribution to the final victory flying night intruder missions.

A number of combat-experienced officers gather around Capt Scott's Black Widow soon after it had scored the 426th's first kill. Standing, from left to right, are Capts Lorne Reynolds, Scott, and Wilfong, an unidentified individual and 426th CO, Maj William Hellriegel. Kneeling, second from right, is Squadron Operations Officer Maj Robert Hamric (*George Porter*)

APPENDICES

CONFIRMED P-61 NIGHT FIGHTER KILLS

6th Night Fighter Squadron (16 kills)

Haberman / Mooney	*MOONHAPPY*	4 'Bettys'
Eaton / Ketchum	*"Jap Batty"*	2 'Bettys'
McCumber / Hinz	*"Midnight Mickey"*.	2 'Bettys'
Thomas / Acre	*"SLEEPY TIME GAL"*	2 'Bettys'
Evans / DeVita		2 'Bettys'
Hansen / Wallace		1 'Betty'
Crumley / Desclos		1 'Betty'
Ferguson / Ward	*THE VIRGIN WIDOW*	1 'Betty'
Szpila / Borges		1 'Frances'

414th Night Fighter Squadron (5 kills)

Jones / Rudovsky.	1 Me 410, 1 Ju 88, 1 Ju 87
Goodrich / Lanes.	1 Ju88
Greenfield / Swartz.	1 Ju52

415th Night Fighter Squadron (0 kills in P-61)

416th Night Fighter Squadron (0 kills in P-61)

417th Night Fighter Squadron (0 kills in P-61)

418th Night Fighter Squadron (18 kills)

Smith / Porter	*'Times A Wastin'*	2 'Irvings'
		1 'Frank'
		1 'Dinah'
		1 'Rufe'
Tompkins / Wertin		2 'Tonys'
		1 floatplane
Sorbo / Kerstette		2 'Jakes'
		1 'Val'
McQueen / Gordon		2 'Tess'
Griffitts / Bigler		1 'Bettys'
Whittern / Crain		1 'Tess'
Ross / Duethman		1 'Betty'
Ritchie / Wertin		1 'Tony'
Ellings / Burman		1 'Rufe'

419th Night Fighter Squadron (5 kills)

Lucas / Blankenship	1 'Sally'
Schroth / James	1 'Dinah'
Dessert / Thompson	1 'Dinah'
LeVitt / Kahn	1 'Betty'
Michels / Morgan	1 'Nick'

421st Night Fighter Squadron (13 Kills)

Wolf / Allain	*Dame de la Nuit*	3 Zekes
		1 'Sally'
Bjorum / Williams		1 'Betty'
		1 'Dinah'
Lockard / Thornton		2 'Tonys'
Pahlka / Hulsey		1 'Helen'
Jones / Woodring		1 'Frank'
Smith / Bremer		1 Zeke
Pew / Cutshall		1 Zeke
Remington / Boze		1 'Betty'

422nd Night Fighter Squadron (43 kills)

Ernst / Kopsel	*"BORROWED TIME"*	3 Ju 87s	
		1 Ju 188	
		1 Bf 110	
Smith / Tierney	*"Lady Gen"*	2 Ju 188s	
		1 Me 410	
		1 Ju 88	
		1 He 111	
Axtell / Orzel	*'Battle Ax'*	2 Ju 188s	
		2 Ju 52s	
		1 Ju 88	
Elmore / Mapes	*"SHOO-SHOO-BABY"*	2 Ju 52s	
		1 Bf 110	
		1 Ju 88	
Bolinder / Graham	*"DOUBLE TROUBLE"*	2 He 111s	
		1 Bf 110	
		1 Fw 190	
Gordon / Crew		1 Ju 88,	
		1 Ju 52	
Gordon / Morrison		1 Ju 188	
J Anderson / Mogan	*TENNESSEE "RIDGE RUNNER"*	2 Ju 88s	
R Anderson / Morris		1 He 111	
		1 Ju 88	
R Anderson / Graham		1 Do 217	
O Johnson / Montgomery	*'No Love, No Nothing'*	1 Fw 190	
		1 Ju 188	
Romens / Morin		1 Ju 88	
Burleson / Monahan		1 Bf110	
Spelis / Eleftherion...	*'Katy The Kid'*	1 Bf 110	
		1 Ju 88	
Koehler / Bost	*"SLEEPY TIME GAL"*	2 Do 217s	
T Jones / Adams		1 Fw 190	
		1 Ju 52	
Burnett / Brandt		1 Ju 52	
Merriman / Dow		1 Ju 52	

425th Night Fighter Squadron (10 kills)

Ormsby / Howerton		1 Do 217
		1 Bf 110
		1 Ju 188
Andrews / Kleinheinz		2 Ju 88s
Slayton / Ferris		1 Bf 110
Slayton / Robinson		1 Ju 188
Sartanowicz / Van Sickels		1 Ju 87
Stacey / Mason		1 Ju 88
Gray / Robinson		1 Ju 188

426th Night Fighter Squadron (5 kills)

Absmeier / Smith	*Jing Bow Joy Ride*	2 'Lilys'
Wilfong / Ashley	*"I'll get By"*	1 'Dinah'
Heise / Brock		1 'Lily'
Scott / Phillips	*Merry-Widow*	1 'Lily'

427th Night Fighter Squadron (0 kills in P-61)

547th Night Fighter Squadron (6 kills)

Bourque / Rucks	*Swing Shift Skipper*	2 'Bettys'
Schreiber / Rucks		1 'Tess'
Blackman / Harper		1 'Tess'
Oakes / Jacqmin		1 'Tess'
Annis / Detz		1 'Hamp'

548th Night Fighter Squadron (5 kills)

Shepherd / Schulenburger	*Midnite Miss*	1 'Tojo'
Dames / D'Andrea	*BAT OUTA HELL II*	1 'Rufe'
Bradford / Lunt	*MIDNITE MADNESS II*	1 'Betty'
Bertram / Fairweather	*Hanger Lil*	1 'Betty'
Schultz / Hill		1 'Betty'

549th Night Fighter Squadron (1 kill)

Gendreau / Chiappinelli	1 'Betty'

550th Night Fighter Squadron (0 kills in P-61)

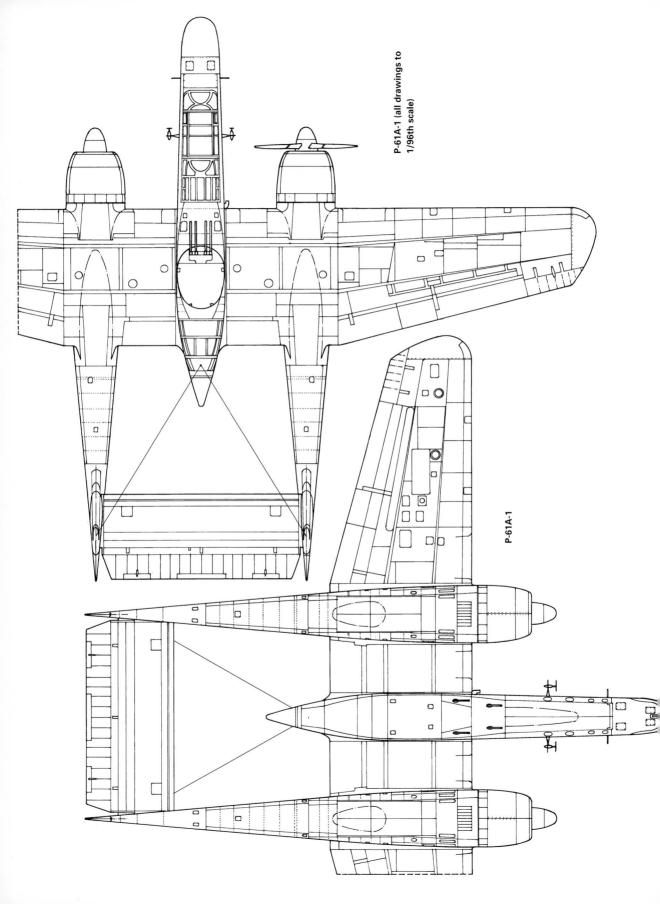

P-61A-1 (all drawings to 1/96th scale)

P-61A-1

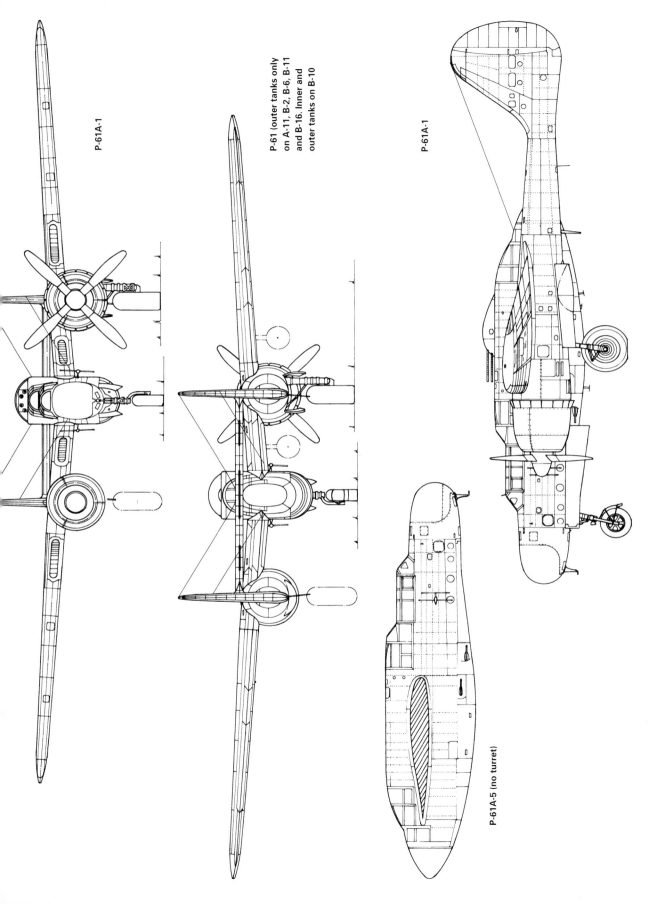

P-61A-1

P-61 (outer tanks only on A-11, B-2, B-6, B-11 and B-16. Inner and outer tanks on B-10

P-61A-1

P-61A-1

P-61A-5 (no turret)

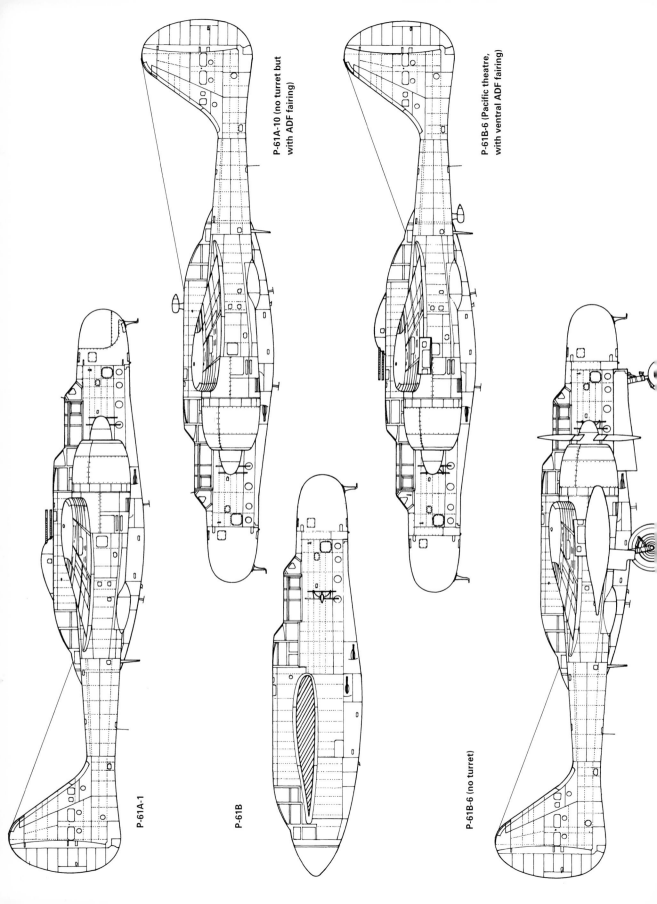

P-61A-10 (no turret but with ADF fairing)

P-61B-6 (Pacific theatre, with ventral ADF fairing)

P-61A-1

P-61B

P-61B-6 (no turret)

1
P-61A-1 42-5524 *"Midnight Mickey"*, crewed by 2Lt Myrle McCumber, R/O Flt Off Daniel Hinz and Gunner Pvt Peter Dutkanicz, 6th NFS, Saipan, mid-1944

2
P-61A-1 44-5528 *"Jap Batty"*, crewed by 1Lt Francis Eaton, R/O 2Lt James Ketchum and Gunner S/Sgt William Anderson, 6th NFS, Saipan, November 1944

3
P-61A-1 42-5502 *"Skippy"*, crewed by 2Lt David Corts and R/O Lt Alexander Berg, 421st NFS, Tacloban Strip, Leyte, late 1944

4
P-61A-5 42-5547 *"BORROWED TIME"*, crewed by 1Lt Herman Ernst and R/O 2Lt Edward Kopsel, 422nd NFS, Ford, England, July 1944

5
P-61A-5 42-5564 *JUKIN' Judy*, crewed by Lt Eugene Lee and R/O Lt Donald Doyle, 422nd NFS, Etain, France, late 1944

6
P-61A-5 42-5544 *"Lady GEN"*, crewed by Lt Paul A Smith and R/O Lt Robert Tierney, 422nd NFS, Florennes, Belgium, late December 1944

7
P-61A-1 44-5526 *NIGHTIE MISSION*, 6th NFS, Saipan, mid-1944

8
P-61A-1 44-5527 *MOONHAPPY*, crewed by 2Lt Dale 'Hap' Haberman, R/O Lt Raymond Mooney and Gunner Pvt Pat Farelly, 6th NFS, Saipan, late 1944

9
P-61A-5 42-5554 *THE VIRGIN WIDOW*, crewed by 2Lt Robert Ferguson, R/O 2Lt Charles Ward and Gunner Sgt Leroy Miozzi, 6th NFS, Saipan, late December 1944

10
P-61A-10 42-5598 *"SLEEPY TIME GAL" II*, crewed by Lt Ernest R Thomas and R/O 2Lt John P Acre, 6th NFS, Saipan, early 1945

11
P-61A-10 42-5565 *"DOUBLE TROUBLE"*, crewed by 2Lt Robert G Bolinder and R/O Flt Off Robert F Graham, 422nd NFS, Etain, France, late 1944

12
P-61B-15 42-39672 *"Little Audrey"*, 422nd NFS, Etain, France, late 1944

13
P-61A-10 42-5576 *SLEEPY TIME GAL*, 425th NFS, Coloummiers, France, Autumn 1944

14
P-61A-10 42-5580 *WABASH CANNON-BALL IV*, crewed by Squadron Commanding Officer Lt Col Leon G 'Gilly' Lewis and Senior Squadron R/O Lt Karl W Soukikian, 425th NFS, Coloummiers, France, Autumn 1944

15
P-61A-10 42-5569 *TABITHA*, crewed by Lt Bruce Heflin and R/O Flt Off William B Broach, 425th NFS, Vannes, France, October 1944

16
P-61A-10 42-5616 *Merry-Widow*, crewed by Capt Robert R Scott and R/O Flt Off Charles W Phillips, 426th NFS, Kunming, China, late October 1944

17
P-61A-10 42-5619 *SATAN 13*, flown by Capt John Pemberton, 426th NFS, Kunming (and other forward strips), China, Autumn 1944

18
P-61A-10 42-39365 *Black-Jack*, flown by 1Lt Glen E Jackson, 426th NFS, Chengtu, China, late 1944

19
P-61A-10 42-5626 *Jing-Bow Joy-Ride*, crewed by Capt Carl J Absmeier and R/O Lt James R Smith, 426th NFS, Chengtu, China, February 1945

20
P-61B-1 42-39417 *THE GREAT SPECKLED BIRD*, crewed by Squadron Maintenance Officer Lt Dick Hoover and Senior Squadron R/O Lt Earl R Dickey, 416th NFS, Horsching, Austria, June 1945

21
P-61A-10 42-5591 *"Impatient WIDOW"*, 422nd NFS, Etain, France, late 1944

22
P-61A-5 42-5534 *"SHOO-SHOO-BABY"*, crewed by Lt Robert O Elmore and R/O Lt Leonard F Mapes, 422nd NFS, Chateaudun, France, Autumn 1944

23
P-61A-10 42-5573 *"Lovely Lady"*, 422nd NFS, Etain, France, late 1944

24
P-61A-10 42-5615 *"I'll get By"*, crewed by Capt John J Wilfong and R/O 2Lt Glenn E Ashley, 426th NFS, Kunming, China, November 1944

25
P-61B-6 42-39514 *HEL'N BACK* , 416th NFS, Horsching, Austria, June 1945

26
P-61B-2 42-39408 *Lady in the Dark*, crewed by Capt Sol Solomon and R/O Lt John Scheerer, 548th NFS, Iwo Jima, Spring 1945

27
P-61B-1 42-39450, 419th NFS, Zamboanga, Mindanao Island, the Philippines, early 1945

28
P-61B-6 42-39527 *BLIND DATE*, flown by Lt Milton Green, 549th NFS, Iwo Jima, early 1945

29
P-61A-10 42-5623 *Sweatin'Wally*, flown by Capt Walter A Storck, 427th NFS, Myitkyina, Burma, late 1944

30
P-61B-2 42-39454 *Cooper's Snooper*, flown by 1Lt George C Cooper, 548th NFS, Iwo Jima, Spring 1945

31
P-61B-1 42-39440 *Swing Shift Skipper*, crewed by 1Lt Arthur D Bourque and R/O 2Lt Bonnie B Rucks, 547th NFS, Lingayen, Luzon, the Philippines, February 1945

32
P-61B-6 42-39504 *MIDNIGHT MADONNA*, flown by both Lt Donald W Weichlein and Lt Frank L Williams, 549th NFS, Saipan, early 1945

33
P-61B-6 42-39525 *night TAKE-OFF*, 548th NFS, Iwo Jima, Spring 1945

34
P-61A-11 42-5609 *BAT OUTA HELL*, flown by Squadron Operations Officer Capt Bill Dames, 548th NFS, Kipapa Gulch, Hawaii, October 1944

35
P-61B-1 42-39405 *Victory Model/"ANONYMOUS" III/The SPOOK*, crewed by Lt Melvin Bode and R/O Lt Avery J Miller, 548th NFS, Iwo Jima, April 1945

36
P-61A-11 42-5610 *MiDNiTE MADNESS*, crewed by Capt James W Bradford, R/O Lt Larry Lunt and Gunner M/Sgt Reno Sukow, 548th NFS, Iwo Jima, April 1945

37
P-61B-2 42-39428 *OUR PANTHER*, crewed by 2Lt Fred M Kuykendall, R/O Flt Off Charles H Rouse and Gunner Cpl George Bancroft, 548th NFS, Ie Shima, Spring 1945

Artist Profile – Sgt L F Miozzi, Gunner, 6th NFS (interviewed by Mark Styling)

Of the nose arts depicted in the colour section of this volume, LeRoy F Miozzi painted *"Midnight Mickey"*, *NIGHT-IE MISSION*, *"Jap Batty"*, *MOONHAPPY* and *THE VIRGIN WIDOW* of the 6th NFS (his unit), and *Lady in the Dark* of the 548th NFS. He produced the paintings by enlarging a sketch using a grid system drawn with chalk ordinarily employed by Operations personnel to announce mission details. Miozzi's grid would consist of a series of six-inch boxes, each of which represented a half-inch box on his original sketch. This system allowed him to accurately reproduce the pin up art so popular with USAAF crews at the time, Miozzi creating his nose art using whatever paint he could get his hands on, applied with brushes sent to him from home.

The basic colours available on Saipan were red, blue and yellow, together with black and white. Mozzi would mix these paints to give some variety, creating a flesh tone, for example, by mixing red with white. Working on the ramp, he used a stand to gain the required height and rigged up an awning to protect himself from the tropical sun, as each painting took between four to six hours to complete – Operations staff would not permit the use of hangars for such trivial undertakings as the painting of nose art.

Rather than shading a picture with colour, he used flat tones outlined in black to give a cartoon effect. Further use of black paint in sparing amounts added extra shading, thus giving the picture form. Finally, Miozzi faithfully recreated various fonts in order to complement the professional quality of his nose art. His services were greatly in demand, and he was paid for his efforts – payment ranged from a bottle of Bourbon to $100 for a B-29 nose art, each crewmember of the Boeing bomber chipping in $10 apiece to secure the commission!

After the war Miozzi became a jewellery designer, his work being marketed by Tiffany and other leading fashion houses. LeRoy Miozzi has helped ensure that each of the nose arts depicted in this volume are faithful to his original by recalling the colours he used 54 years ago – such is his memory that despite the intervening years, he still remembers that the jewel on *MOONHAPPY*'s skirt was bright yellow!

1

P-61A-1 42-5524 *"Midnight Mickey"*, crewed by 2Lt Myrle McCumber, R/O Flt Off Daniel Hinz and Gunner Pvt Peter Dutkanicz, 6th NFS, Saipan, mid-1944

This aircraft was one of the first production A-models delivered by Northrop, as denoted by its olive drab paint scheme. Its assigned crew were credited with two confirmed kills (both 'Bettys') whilst flying this aircraft. The lower radome of this aircraft has been liberally covered with grey lead paint in order to reduce the levels of ground clutter picked up by its radar – virtually all early P-61A-1s were so decorated. The darker shade of green on the aircraft's rudders was caused by the olive drab fading more slowly on the control surfaces.

2

P-61A-1 44-5526 *NIGHTIE MISSION*, 6th NFS, Saipan, mid-1944

This aircraft was one of the most elaborately painted P-61As to see service in any theatre, its artwork being applied by Gunner Sgt L F Miozzi. Amongst the handful of olive drab aircraft delivered to the 6th NFS, it too boasted the grey strip on the base of its radome.

3

P-61A-1 44-5528 *"Jap Batty"*, crewed by 1Lt Francis Eaton, R/O 2Lt James Ketchum and Gunner S/Sgt William Anderson, 6th NFS, Saipan, November 1944

This early P-61A-1 was turned over to the 6th NFS at John Rogers Field, Hawaii, in May 1944, the aircraft having been the penultimate A-1 built in a production run that totalled just 45 airframes.

4

P-61A-1 44-5527 *MOONHAPPY*, crewed by 2Lt Dale 'Hap' Haberman, R/O Lt Raymond Mooney and Gunner Pvt Pat Farelly, 6th NFS, Saipan, late 1944

This P-61 was the top 'killer' of the 6th NFS, its crew claiming four confirmed victories. Like the previous aircraft featured on this page, 42-5527 was part of the 45-strong A-1 production run. Its artwork was again by Sgt LeRoy Miozzi.

5

P-61A-5 42-5554 *THE VIRGIN WIDOW*, crewed by 2Lt Robert Ferguson, R/O 2Lt Charles Ward and Gunner Sgt LeRoy Miozzi, 6th NFS, Saipan, late December 1944

This aircraft was one of the first all-black P-61s used by the 6th NFS, its serial indicating that it was a P-61A-5 – part of the second production series to come off the line, there were 35 'Dash 5s' produced. The dorsal turret was deleted during early P-61 production due to both buffeting problems caused when it was rotated in flight and the need for turrets to equip new-build B-29s. Units in the Pacific nevertheless mounted four fixed forward-firing .50

cal machine guns on a frame above the fuselage and faired them over with the standard turret covering, resulting in an arrangement identical to that fitted to earlier turret-equipped models. Miozzi painted through the word *VIRGIN* and the cluster of cherries to the let of the nose art following the aircraft's 'Betty' kill on the night of 26 December 1944.

6

P-61A-1 42-5502 *"Skippy"*, crewed by 2Lt David Corts and R/O Lt Alexander Berg, 421st NFS, Tacloban Strip, Leyte, late 1944

This crew/aircraft combination was credited with the 421st NFS's first kill – and they didn't even have to fire a shot!

7

P-61A-5 42-5543 *TENNESSEE "RIDGE RUNNER"*, crewed by Lt John W Anderson and R/O Lt James W Mogan, 422nd NFS, Chateaudun, France, Autumn 1944

This aircraft was named by its pilot, John W Anderson, who hailed from the mountains east of Tennessee. He teamed up with Mogan to shoot down two Ju 88s on the nights of 24 and 25 December 1944. Note the addition of de-icing boots on the fin and wing leading edges, plus the lack of invasion stripes – nightfighters were specifically exempt from wearing these high-visibility markings.

8

P-61A-5 42-5534 *"SHOO-SHOO-BABY"*, crewed by Lt Robert O Elmore and R/O Lt Leonard F Mapes, 422nd NFS, Chateaudun, France, Autumn 1944

This particular P-61A-5 was one of the most successful nocturnal hunters in western Europe, its crew using it to score four confirmed kills over manned German aircraft – its tally included one Bf 110, one Ju 88, two Ju 52s and a V1. This aircraft was later resprayed in overall gloss black, as shown in the nose art gallery.

9

P-61A-10 42-5598 *"SLEEPY TIME GAL" II*, crewed by Lt Ernest R Thomas and R/O 2Lt John P Acre, 6th NFS, Saipan, early 1945

This aircraft was one of the earliest P-61A-10s issued to the 6th NFS, Northrop manufacturing 100 A-model 'Dash 10s'. Its assigned crew contributed two confirmed kills to the total of 16 scored by the 6th during its time with the P-61. Most Black Widow units boasted an aircraft christened 'Sleepy Time Gal'.

10

P-61A-5 42-5544 *"Lady GEN"*, crewed by Lt Paul A Smith and R/O Lt Robert Tierney, 422nd NFS, Florennes, Belgium, late December 1944

The 'Dash 5s' were the first P-61 to reach both the 422nd and 425th NFSs, swiftly followed by 'Dash 10s'. It was the earlier model aircraft, however, that scored the bulk of the aerial kills in the ETO, the crew of this aircraft, for example, becoming aces. Of the four crews to achieve 'acedom' in the Black Widow, three hailed from the 422nd. This profile at last accurately shows "Lady GEN" in the olive drab scheme that it wore into 1945.

11

P-61B-6 42-39514 *HEL'N BACK*, 416th NFS, Horsching, Austria, June 1945

Some 47 B-model 'Dash 6s' were built, most, if not all of them being issued to NFSs in the MTO. This aircraft was assigned to the 416th NFS as a replacement for the unit's Mosquitos, although the first P-61 did not arrive until the final weeks of the war. Like the P-61A-1, the B-2, -6 and -11 models had outer wing pylons which enabled them to carry either external tanks or bombs. The B-10 introduced an extra pylon under each wing inboard of the engines, this modification being performed in the field.

12

P-61B-1 42-39417 *THE GREAT SPECKLED BIRD*, crewed by Squadron Maintenance Officer Lt Dick Hoover and Senior Squadron R/O Lt Earl R Dickey, 416th NFS, Horsching, Austria, June 1945

This colourful aircraft was assigned to the 416th NFS soon after VE-Day, the unit replacing its Mosquito NF 30s with new P-61B-1s (of which just 62 were built). It would perform most of its flying out of Horsching airfield during the early months of the Allied Occupation of Europe.

13

P-61B-15 42-39606 *"LI'L ABNER"*, crewed by Lt Alvin G Moore and R/O Lt Juan D Lujan, 415th NFS, St Dizier, France, March 1945

This aircraft served with two units in a very short space of time, initially being issued to the 415th NFS in March 1945, before transferring to the 417th NFS after VE-Day. The B-15 saw the reintroduction of the Type A-4 turret.

14

P-61A-10 42-5565 *"DOUBLE TROUBLE"*, crewed by 2Lt Robert G Bolinder and R/O Flt Off Robert F Graham, 422nd NFS, Etain, France, late 1944

This aircraft was one of the first of 100 P-61A-10s to come off the assembly line.

15

P-61A-5 42-5564 *JUKIN' Judy* of Lt Eugene Lee and R/O Lt Donald Doyle, 422nd NFS, Etain, France, late 1944

Assigned to the 422nd NFS when the unit was based at Scorton, in England, this P-61A-5 was the 35th, and final, 'Dash 5' to come off the Northrop line in California. Most early A-5s boasted turrets and were issued to units in the Pacific.

16

P-61B-6 42-39533 *Markey/HADE'S LADY*, 417th NFS,

Giebelstadt and Braunschardt, Germany, June 1945

The 417th NFS remained equipped with Beaufighter VI/VIIIs until war's end, when they were replaced by P-61B-6s. The unit's Black Widows were employed flying mundane patrols over occupied Germany for much of the summer of 1945. This particular aircraft was one of two bought for the USAAF by Northrop workers, one of whom selected the name *Hade's Lady*.

17

P-61B-15 42-39672 *"Little Audrey"*, 422nd NFS, Etain, France, late 1944

This P-61B-15 was one of the few attrition replacements that actually made it to the 422nd NFS following the unit's movement closer to the frontline in France. *"Little Audrey"* was also unusual in that it had additional nose art – most P-61s within the squadron boasted names only.

18

P-61A-10 42-5591 *"Impatient WIDOW"*, 422nd NFS, Etain, France, late 1944

This P-61 was part of the second batch of Black Widows sent to join the 422nd NFS in England soon after the invasion of Normandy. It was later severely damaged in clash with a German nightfighter over France, losing its right engine. In the resulting emergency landing the P-61's nose gear collapsed, putting the aircraft out of service for several days.

19

P-61A-10 42-5573 *"Lovely Lady"*, flown by Lt Donald Show, 422nd NFS, Etain, France, late 1944

The eighth 'Dash 10' to come off the assembly line, this aircraft, like most other P-61s in this batch, was sent to the ETO (the 422nd or 425th primarily). *"Lovely Lady"* finished the war with two kills to its credit.

20

P-61B-1 42-39450, crewed by Lt Phil Hans, R/O Lt 'Doc' Holloway and Gunner Sgt Don Clancy, 419th NFS, Zamboanga, Mindanao Island, the Philip-pines, early 1945

The 419th NFS adopted a more conservative approach to nose art that its contemporaries, restricting personal embellishments to girls' names only. This P-61B-1 was the exception to the rule, however, lacking a name but boasting female-inspired artwork instead.

21

P-61A-10 42-5580 *WABASH CANNON-BALL IV*, crewed by Squadron Commanding Officer Lt Col Leon G 'Gilly' Lewis and Senior Squadron R/O Lt Karl W Soukikian, 425th NFS, Coloummiers, France, Autumn 1944

This P-61A-10 was claimed by 425th NFS CO Maj Leon 'Gilly' Lewis as his personal mount soon after its arrival in England in late June 1944.

22

P-61A-10 42-5576 *SLEEPY TIME GAL*, 425th NFS, Coloummiers, France, Autumn 1944

As with the other 'Dash 5s and 10s' delivered to the 425th NFS in the wake of Operation *Overlord*, this aircraft wears full invasion stripes on its wings and beneath its tail booms.

23

P-61A-10 42-5569 *TABITHA*, crewed by Lt Bruce Heflin and R/O Flt Off William B Broach, 425th NFS, Vannes, France, October 1944

This aircraft had arguably the best nose art of any 425th NFS P-61, and as a result it became the most photo-graphed Black Widow in the unit. Sadly, it was lost in action with its crew on 24 October 1944.

24

P-61A-10 42-5615 *"I'll get By"*, crewed by Capt John J Wilfong and R/O 2Lt Glenn E Ashley, 426th NFS, Kunming, China, November 1944

This 'Dash 10' scored a kill on 21 November 1944 – one of five claimed during the 426th NFS's most successful night of the war.

25

P-61A-10 42-5619 *SATAN 13*, crewed by Capt John Pemberton, R/O Flt Off C W Phillips and Engineer P D Curran, 426th NFS, Kunming, China, late 1944

This aircraft was just one of many A-models completed without a top turret. The oval housing on the spine of the aircraft contained the ADF aerial, this radio directional finding equipment being unique to P-61s in the Pacific and CBI. ADF proved to be critical in both theatres, as crews would often return from long patrols with little fuel reserves and needing precision guidance back to base.

26

P-61A-10 42-5616 *Merry-Widow*, crewed by Capt Robert R Scott and R/O Flt Off Charles W Phillips, 426th NFS, Kunming, China, late October 1944

This P-61A-10 gained the distinction of being the first Black Widow to down an enemy aircraft, its crew claiming a 'Lily' on 29 October 1944.

27

P-61B-1 42-39440 *Swing Shift Skipper*, crewed by 1Lt Arthur D Bourque and R/O 2Lt Bonnie B Rucks, 547th NFS, Lingayen, Luzon, the Philippines, February 1945

This aircraft was the leading scorer for the 547th NFS during its Black Widow era, its crew claiming two 'Betty' bombers destroyed.

28

P-61A-10 42-39365 *Black-Jack*, flown by 1Lt Glen E Jackson, 426th NFS, Chengtu, China, late 1944

This unit received ADF-equipped P-61s while still at Madhaiganj, in India, the first aircraft arriving on 25 September 1944. After establishing its HQ at Chengtu, the 426th operated two/three-aircraft dets from Hsian, Kunming, Liangshan and Ankang.

29

P-61A-5 42-5547 *"BORROWED TIME"*, crewed by 1Lt Herman Ernst and R/O 2Lt Edward Kopsel, 422nd NFS, Ford, England, July 1944

One of the few Black Widows to achieve 'acedom', this aircraft was used by its crew to down five manned aircraft and one V1. For a very brief period just prior to it being written off in an accident, *"BORROWED TIME"* wore shark's teeth painted onto an all-yellow nose – it nose wheel door was also adorned with a Varga pin-up girl.

30

P-61A-11 42-5610 *MiDNiTE MADNESS* of Capt James W Bradford, R/O Lt Larry Lunt and Gunner M/Sgt Reno Sukow, 548th NFS, Iwo Jima, 4/45

The 548th NFS took great pride in the abilities of its artist, and his creations rivalled those of the 6th NFS. The artwork seen here on *MiDNiTE MADNESS* was actually painted on two different P-61s, as this machine (the first 'MADNESS') was destroyed on Iwo Jima in a landing accident caused by heavy ground fog – using the same stencil, the artist did, however, employ different colours on P-61B-1 42-39404 *MiDNiTE MADNESS II*.

31

P-61B-2 42-39428 *OUR PANTHER*, crewed by 2Lt Fred M Kuykendall, R/O Flt Off Charles H Rouse and Gunner Cpl George Bancroft, 548th NFS, Ie Shima, Spring 1945

One of 38 'Dash 2s' built, this aircraft was amongst the first batch of replacement P-61s to reach the 548th NFS. Its artwork was worn on both sides of the nose, and had been applied using a stencil.

32

P-61B-2 42-39408 *Lady in the Dark*, crewed by Capt Sol Solomon and R/O Lt John Scheerer, 548th NFS, Iwo Jima, Spring 1945

Arguably the most famous P-61 of them all, this aircraft was initially flown by pilot Capt Solomon and R/O Lt Scheerer. However, by this late stage of the war there were an excess of aircrews, so P-61s were flown by numerous individuals. For example, Lt Robert W Clyde and R/O Lt Bruce K LeFord flew *'Lady* on a mission performed on the last night of the war, locking on to a Japanese 'Oscar' and chasing it down to wave-top level. The enemy aircraft duly hit the water and exploded before a shot was fired, leading some historians to state that this might have been the last aerial kill of World War 2.

33

P-61B-6 42-39525 *night TAKE-OFF*, 548th NFS, Iwo Jima, Spring 1945

This P-61B-6 was part of the second major shipment of replacement aircraft sent to the Pacific, most of which were assigned to the 549th NFS, rather than the 548th.

34

P-61B-2 42-39454 *Cooper's Snooper* of 1Lt George C

Cooper, 548th NFS, Iwo Jima, Spring 1945

This P-61 was adorned with nose art painted by the same artist that had decorated 42-39525.

35

P-61B-1 42-39405 *Victory Model/"ANONYMOUS" III/The SPOOK*, crewed by Lt Melvin Bode and R/O Lt Avery J Miller, 548th NFS, Iwo Jima, April 1945

Like 42-5610, this P-61B-1 was the first of two Black Widows to be adorned with this nose art, both of which were assigned to the 548th NFS's Lt. Mel Bode and R/O Lt Avery Miller.

36

P-61A-11 42-5609 *BAT OUTA HELL* of Squadron Operations Officer Capt Bill Dames, R/O 2Lt E P D'Andrea and Gunner Sgt R C Ryder, 48th NFS, Kipapa Gulch, Hawaii, October 1944

The first of two *BAT OUTA HELLs*, this aircraft was one of the first 48th NFS P-61s to receive nose art at Kipapa Gulch. It was subsequently lost in an accident and a second Black Widow so painted, although with slightly different nose art.

37

P-61A-10 42-5626 *Jing-Bow Joy-Ride*, crewed by Capt Carl J Absmeier and R/O Lt James R Smith, 426th NFS, Chengtu, China, February 1945

This P-61A-10 was the leading scorer in the 426th, shooting down two 'Lily' bombers. 'Jing Bow' were the Chinese words for 'Air Raid'.

38

P-61B-6 42-39504 *MIDNIGHT MADONNA*, flown by both Lt Donald W Weichlein and Lt Frank L Williams, 549th NFS, Saipan, early 1945

Few 549th NFS aircraft received elaborate nose art, this aircraft being the exception.

39

P-61A-10 42-5623 *Sweatin'Wally*, flown by Capt Walter A Storck, 427th NFS, Myitkyina, Burma, late 1944

This P-61A-10s was part of a substantial shipment sent to a large reassembly centre in India, prior to being issued to either of the frontline units.

40

P-61B-6 42-39527 *BLIND DATE*, flown by Lt Milton Green, 549th NFS, Iwo Jima, early 1945

This aircraft spent most of its combat tenure flying from Iwo Jima after March 1945. Note the attachment points for underwing rocket rails.

Back Cover

P-61B-6 42-39532 *First Nighter*, flown by Capt Joe Jenkins, 414th NFS, Pontedera, Italy, late 1944

The second P-61 purchased by the Northrop work-ers, it was named by employee A A Johnson.

FIGURE PLATES

1

John W Myers, Chief P-61 Test Pilot at Northrop's Hawthorne plant in California in 1944-45. Although strictly a civilian, he is predominantly clothed in military-issue apparel, including a one-piece lightweight overall and HS-38 headset (Type ANB-H-1 receivers) with throat microphone. Myers' has a B-8 parachute pack slung over his left shoulder, whilst his russet brown shoes also appear to be standard USAAF officers' issue. Finally, his baseball cap is of civilian origin, for it has the Northrop logo woven onto its front.

2

Lt John W Anderson served as a pilot with the 422nd NFS at Chateaudun, in France, during 1944/45. He is wearing the classical USAAF ETO fighter pilot's combination of lightweight khaki 'pinks' (uniform khaki trousers), a matching open-necked shirt and a personalised A-2 leather jacket – note the 422nd NFS circular patch obscured by his left hand. Over his A-2, Anderson has a B-8 parachute harness secured across his chest, although the leg straps remain undone because the actual 'chute is missing. His headwear consists of a highly-prized ex-RAF issue Type C helmet, devoid of goggles.

3

Lt Leonard F Mapes, radar observer with the 422nd NFS at Chateaudun in the autumn of 1944, wears standard issue 'pinks', russet brown shoes and a B-8 parachute harness, again devoid of a 'chute. Like Anderson, his helmet is an ex-RAF Type C, paired with a USAAF issue A-10 mask and Type B-8 goggles, made by Polaroid.

4

Lt Al Innerarity, radar observer with the 425th NFS at Vannes, in France, September 1944. He is wearing an AN-S-31 summer flying suit, over which he has donned his favourite A-2 jacket. A silk scarf around his neck prevents chafing against the cotton/wool gabardine overall. Innerarity's hands are protected by B-2 summer gloves, and he has a B-8 parachute harness (devoid of the 'chute) secured to his upper torso. Finally, his uniform is completed with a standard service cap that has had its crown stiffener spring removed in order to obtain the much desired '50 mission crush' look.

5

2Lt Jean B Desclos (radar observer) served with the 6th NFS on Saipan in 1944/45. As with Innerarity, Desclos is wearing a Suit, Summer, Flying, AN-3-31A, although his example (khaki coloured) is made of lightweight cotton twill, which was more suited to the heat of the tropics. He has an S-1 lifejacket around his neck, an AN-H-15 helmet and Type B-8 goggles on his head and a hunting knife on his hip. Standard issue US Army QMC boots complete Desclos' uniform.

6

2Lt James Postlewaite (pilot) of the 422nd NFS at Maupertus (A-15), France, in July 1944. Once again attired in the ubiquitous AN-3-31A (thicker cotton/wool gabardine garment), Postlewaite wears a B-4 lifejacket and the B-8 parachute harness, although unlike previous examples seen in these plates, he has his crotch straps done up. Positioned at a suitably jaunty angle is the pilot's standard issue '50 mission crush' service cap.